Heaven, We Have a Problem

Heaven, We Have a Problem
13 Miracles from the Apollo 13 Mission That Will Rocket Your Faith

by David Myers

Fitly Spoken Press

Heaven, We Have a Problem: 13 Miracles from the Apollo 13 Mission That Will Rocket Your Faith
Published by Fitly Spoken Press
1021 Emerson Drive NE
Palm Bay, FL 32907 USA

Copyright © 2014 by David Myers

All rights reserved. No part of this book may be reproduced, stored in a retrieval system, or transmitted in any form or by any means without the written permission of the publisher.

Printed in the United States of America

ISBN: 978-0-9836707-2-8

Cover design by Judy Brown.

All Scripture quotations, unless otherwise indicated, are taken from the *Holy Bible, New International Version®. NIV®.* Copyright © 1973, 1978, 1984 by International Bible Society. Used by permission of Zondervan. All rights reserved.

Scripture verses marked KJV are from the King James Version of the Bible.

DISCLAIMER AND/OR LEGAL NOTICES
While the publisher and author have used their best efforts in preparing this book, they make no representations or warranties with respect to the accuracy or completeness of the contents of this book. The advice and strategies contained herein may not be suitable for your situation. You should consult a professional where appropriate. Neither the publisher nor the author shall be liable for any loss of profit or any other commercial damages, including but not limited to special, incidental, consequential, or other damages. The purchaser or reader of this publication assumes responsibility for the use of these materials and information. Adherence to all applicable laws and regulations, both advertising and all other aspects of doing business in the United States or any other jurisdiction, is the sole responsibility of the purchaser or reader.

To my heroes—
my father,
ministers and missionaries,
explorers and adventurers,
in this world and the world to come.

Contents

Foreword	*xi*
Acknowledgements	*xix*
Prologue: Eyes on the Sky	**1**
Chapter 1: Malfunction?	**9**
Apollo 13 Miracle #1: Center Engine Cutoff	9
Malfunction, or God-function?	11
From Pain to Promise	12
Hurt	13
Helplessness	14
Preparation	15
Strengthening	15
Prayer	17
Patience and Wisdom	18
Opportunity	20
Chapter 2: The Value of Imperfection	**23**
Apollo 13 Miracle #2: A Faulty Gauge	23
The Imperfect Human Need for Order amid Chaos	24
God Uses Imperfection	29
Chapter 3: All in God's Time	**35**
Apollo 13 Miracle #3: Timing	35
The Original Mission Plan	36
God's Strategic Timing	37
God's Well-Timed Warning System	41
A Life-Saving Early Warning System	43
Chapter 4: Hidden Opportunity	**49**
Apollo 13 Miracle #4: A Malfunctioning Hatch	49
Problems: Closed Doors or Future Opportunities?	50
Closed Doors That Are Miracles Awaiting Audacious Prayer	51
Heartache: An Open Door That We Can't Close Alone	54
Hope: An Open Door That Will Not Close	55
Chapter 5: "There Shall Be Wings!"	**59**
Apollo 13 Miracle #5: Measles	59
God Uses Setbacks as Setups for the Miraculous	61

God Uses Setbacks as Setups for Spiritual Renewal	65
God Gives Each of Us His or Her Own Wings	68
God Gives You Your Wings	72

Chapter 6: Attitude and Guts — 77

Powering Up	77
Apollo 13 Miracle #6: A Gut Feeling	77
"Failure Is Not an Option"	79
Failure Is Not an Option with God	79
Failure Is Not an Option with the Word of God	80
Failure Is Not an Option with the Church	80
Failure Is Not an Option with the Holy Spirit	80
Failure Is Not an Option: The Attitude of Successful Action	81
The Long Way Home	84
Around the Moon	87

Chapter 7: An Empowered Mission — 91

Apollo 13 Miracle #7: *Marooned*	91
Hope = Mission Possible	92
God Empowers Your Mission	95

Chapter 8: Sticky Situations — 101

Apollo 13 Miracle #8: Duct Tape	101
Man's Spiritual "Duct Tape": Stick Relentlessly with God	103

Chapter 9: Guidance System — 113

Apollo 13 Miracle #9: A Navigation Mishap	113
Successful Navigation through Life	114
A Line to Divide Darkness and Light	116
A Line to Divide Death and Life	118

Chapter 10: The Heavenly Rendezvous Approach — 123

Apollo 13 Miracle #10: The Functioning Hatch	123
The Power of *Again*	124
The Strongest Connection	128

Chapter 11: Unshakable — 137

Apollo 13 Miracle #11: The Command Module Wasn't Severed	137
God's Firm Grip	138
It's Liberating to Be Limited	139
Limitations of Our Nature	142

Chapter 12: Silver Linings	**147**
Apollo 13 Miracle #12: Placement of Oxygen Tank Two	147
Tragedy-Inspired Appreciation	148
God's Strategic Plan and Placement	150
The Blessing That Follows the Battle	156
The Tragic Fire That Saved Apollo 13	160
Chapter 13: Divine Asset	**165**
Apollo 13 Miracle #13: The Heat Shield	165
A Spiritual Heat Shield	166
When Explosions Strike	170
Chapter 14: Streets of Gold	**181**
A Successful Failure	181
From Failure to Freedom	181
Freedom to Fill the Road to Heaven	184
Renewal and Revival	185
Our Own "Mission Control Pit Crew"	186
Bibliography	**195**
About the Author	**197**

Foreword

"Houston, we have a problem." This often misquoted Apollo 13 distress call, made famous years later by a popular movie starring Tom Hanks, is almost as famous as Neil Armstrong's "That's one small step for [a] man, one giant leap for mankind." The former is now humorously used for any difficulty we are facing.

Let's be honest. We did not get to the moon without having a few problems to solve. At the height of the Apollo buildup, there were more than 400,000 people working at 21,000 organizations who were devoted to accomplishing this feat. That's a lot of focused manpower. Many years earlier it had only been a dream. In 1961, when John F. Kennedy put forth his challenge of landing a man on the moon by the end of the decade, his inspiring words set things in motion. I think this quote attributed to Goethe sums it up well: "The moment one definitely commits oneself, then providence moves too. All sorts of things occur to help one that would never otherwise have occurred. Whatever you can do, or dream you can, begin it. Boldness has genius, power, and magic in it. Begin it now."

Nothing is ever accomplished without a struggle. It takes brilliant men and women who are not afraid to think big and are willing to fight for their dreams. Albert Einstein once said, "Great spirits have always encountered violent opposition from mediocre minds." If we learn anything from those who have accomplished great things, it's that they were not afraid of **problems**, they were **persistent**, and they were **prepared**.

PROBLEMS: Are you experiencing difficulties? Do you have troubles that seemingly can't be solved? Welcome to the human race. Life as we know it is never easy. We all have problems—even tragedies—to contend with. However, true happiness is not the lack of problems; it's the ability to deal with them. That is why from the day we were born, our parents, teachers, elders, and mentors have tried their very best to prepare us with insight, wisdom, and skills to meet the never-ending challenges that life may throw our way.

PERSISTENCE: I was introduced to the word "persistence" after one of my high school teachers signed my senior yearbook by saying, "John, persevere! Find out what that means and you will succeed in life." Well, to be honest, I had to look it up to understand what she meant. I'm so glad I did. It changed my life! Her advice was worth more than all my school years put together. Nothing in the world can take the place of persistence. Victory may not come until after the fourth or fifth try, so don't ever give up. Don't ever give in. Don't ever stop trying. You haven't failed unless you've surrendered.

We are made to persist. Even if you stumble, you're still moving forward. The sky is not the limit. We are. Shoot for the moon—even if you miss, you will land among the stars. Without fire in the belly (motivation), all talent, training, and knowledge is useless. Don't stop when you are tired—only stop when you are done. Surround yourself with people who believe in the impossible, not those who don't. Focus on your potential, not your limitations.

PREPERATION: When I was a Boy Scout and reading *Boys' Life* magazine as a youth, I was reminded over and over again to always "be prepared." I soon learned this was more than just a slick motto. It was a strategy for living. The best way to face life is to be ready. You won't have to look for challenges—they will find you.

Benjamin Franklin once said, "By failing to prepare, you are preparing to fail." That reminds me of my Navy days. Boot camp was a crash course of how to fit into Navy culture and prepare for emergencies. We learned how to combat shipboard fires, survive toxic gas leaks, and use our blue Navy-issued dungaree shirts as life buoys in case we fell overboard. And to help make men out of momma's boys and lazy brats who hadn't developed a work ethic at home, the Navy had their own version of a drill sergeant. We polished a lot of boots, as well as belt buckles, doorknobs, drains, urinals, light fixtures, window locks, railings—actually anything that appeared to be brass. Everything in the Navy would have Mr. Clean's stamp of approval. To become a squared-away sailor takes a long time. To become a Navy SEAL, much longer.

BUD/S (Basic Underwater Demolition/SEAL) training takes preparation to a whole new level. Hell Week is the demise of many. Going 6 days without sleep, while running more than 200 miles with a 250-pound rubber boat bouncing on top of your head and enduring nonstop physical drills and harassment, isn't exactly a recipe for the faint of heart. Navy SEALs demand the best. Our survival depended on it. One thing that stayed with me, long after my four-year stint with the Underwater Demolition/SEAL team tour ended, was this: Be prepared for the unexpected, and stay calm!

Much of BUD/S training revolved around overcoming obstacles, sucking up excruciating pain, and hanging tough to the very end, no matter what. "The only easy day was yesterday" became our battle cry! A tenacious and unyielding spirit was instilled in me that exists to this day.

Learning SCUBA, parachuting, demolition, and long-distance swimming skills was very important. But we were also trained to deal with the unexpected while doing them. Drown-proofing, for example, involved swimming fifty meters with our hands and feet tied behind our backs. This, we were told, was to inspire confidence, just in case we were tied up and held captive in a Viet Cong sampan, and found a way to escape by sliding into the murky brown water.

SCUBA training was a blast too. That is, if you enjoyed learning how to keep your cool while a couple of instructors were simultaneously shutting off your tank's oxygen valve, pulling off your fins and face mask, unbuckling your weight belt, and releasing the shoulder straps to your tank while you were submerged deep under water. Necessary, they said, to learn not to panic under duress and stay calm enough to fix the problem rather than lose your cool and die. That's more challenging than it sounds, especially when your lungs are screaming for air.

Before each parachute jump, we had to sit through a sobering briefing to remind us how to use a reserve chute just in case the main chute didn't open. You can only imagine how the very thought of such wedged itself in our brains, as we jumped out of the plane into the dark blue sky, several thousand feet above ground. (I think that is where I first learned to thank God—right after hearing the sweet, reassuring sound of silk unraveling above me and seeing a full canopy when I looked up.)

One of the hardest lessons I had to learn was trusting in my fellow man and equipment. Human errors and mechanical breakdowns have killed thousands. I always prayed the guy who packed my parachute wasn't doing this for the very first time, tripping out on LSD, or ticked off at me. A night underwater swim in zero visibility was only successful if I disregarded my human senses that were screaming at me to go in the opposite direction of the very tried and proven illuminated compass, that was embedded in a piece of board held in front of me. Those who didn't master this found themselves swimming 180 degrees in the opposite direction or going in circles. Diving with a closed-circuit mixed-gas rebreather rig could be life threatening if the guys responsible for refilling my tanks hadn't purged them first. I lost five Navy SEAL teammates in Vietnam when their helicopter malfunctioned and crashed. I think you get the picture.

I turned down the opportunity to serve on the rescue mission of Apollo 13 as a recovery swimmer only because I was sick and tired of going through more tedious rehearsals. I had my fill of that while serving on both the Apollo 10 and 11 space missions. The Navy made us go through the recovery process so many times it became a part of our dreams. We could have almost done our job blindfolded. Repetition, though extremely boring, sharpens one's skills to the point of perfection. Everyone on the ship knew his job inside and out. You can't fault the Navy for lack of preparation. Someone way up the chain of command must have been a Boy Scout.

I was the first man in the water to reach the Apollo 11 capsule that early morning of July 24, 1969. My first responsibility, after taking a quick look in the hatch window to see if the astronauts were okay, was to attach a sea anchor to the bobbing craft. If they had known I was only a twenty-year-old kid fresh out of high school, they might not have had such big smiles on their faces. Others who helped attach the flotation collar joined me later. Neil Armstrong, Buzz Aldrin, and Michael Collins were all lifted safely into the rescue helicopter after the decontamination process was completed. Job well done! Credit goes to all for months of preparation and training.

The flotation collar we attached to the *Columbia* became an integral part of all space rescue missions only after Gus Grissom's Mercury capsule, named *Liberty Bell 7*, sank to the bottom of the Atlantic Ocean in 1961. The door blew open prematurely, and a wave of salt water flooded the capsule, taking it down to Davy Jones's locker. Gus almost drowned that day, but fortunately he survived—thus the need for a flotation collar during water recoveries was born. The sunken Mercury capsule was finally recovered in 1999. Fortunately, we humans do learn from our mistakes. Sometimes.

In *Heaven, We Have a Problem*, David Myers shares valuable insights of how to triumph over the unexpected. He shares interesting stories that helped bring the Apollo 13 crew back to Earth safely after facing insurmountable odds. He intertwines these fascinating stories with Biblical truths and principles.

All of us have learned through the years that life sometimes throws a nasty punch. After turning my life over to the Lord and being born again, I discovered another compass to follow—the Word of God and the Lord's abiding Spirit within me. It truly takes faith to trust in God and His Word when life's complexities are bombarding you with fear and doubt. Often I can't see through the dense fog of what seems to be an impossible situation. But I have learned (well, I'm still trying) to stay calm, knowing that *"in all things God works for the good of those who love Him, who have been called according to His purpose" (Romans 8:28b)*.

I have seen many incredible comebacks through my years serving as pastor, evangelist, and missionary. Most rewarding of all is seeing God transform people who have been written off as hopeless cases. If you are a prodigal, come on home! There truly is life after failure, life after disappointment, and life after death. After all, this world is not our home. We are just passing through.

Caution: You are about to get a fresh jolt of encouragement. Myers's insights will cause your faith in God to skyrocket. You are now on the launch pad for a huge boost. Your worries will soon seem smaller and your burdens much lighter. Earth's gravity will soon release its hold on you. You will feel almost weightless as God lifts you up and over troubled waters.

The psalmist must have had days like that when he wrote, *"With Your help I can advance against a troop; with my God I can scale a wall" (Psalm 18:29)*.

So fasten your seatbelt and brace yourself. It's time for blastoff.

—John Wolfram
UDT-11 Apollo 11 rescue swimmer
author of *Splashdown: The Rescue of a Navy Frogman*

Acknowledgements

Heaven, We Have a Problem has benefited from a lot of people who inspired and enhanced the process, some knowingly and others perhaps not knowingly.

My wife and children are a continual source of strength and blessing. I can't imagine life without them.

A special thanks to John for his service and friendship, and to Tammy and Brian for their patience and expertise in bringing this project to life.

The research and analysis of Apollo 13 by Jerry Woodfill revealed the hand of God in a unique way that has increased the faith of many.

Thank you to every hero and heroine who risked and gave their life for the purpose of exploring the heavens and bringing them closer to Earth.

I am grateful for our church family at First Pentecostal Church in Palm Bay, Florida. Your support and faithfulness makes it possible to dream and write.

My parents have been more than just model parents; they have faithfully ministered together for more than fifty years. They continue to encourage by their consistency.

I am thankful to know the best friend that a human could have: Jesus Christ.

Apollo 15 launch. Credit: NASA.

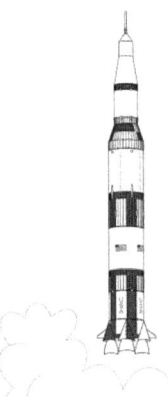

Prologue
Eyes on the Sky

Spring 1971

"David?" My dad briskly rubbed his hands together and smiled down at me, his eyes merry. "You, your sister, your mom, and me—we're going to move. I'm going to be pastor at a small church in Palm Bay. That's on the other side of Florida."

"Move?" I stared up at him, my seven-year-old mind devastated.

Leave Port St. Joe? But this was home! My friends, my school, the beautiful beaches would all be left behind.

My dad leaned closer, like he knew a secret. "Do you know what Palm Bay is near?"

"No. What?"

He leaned even closer and lowered his voice to just above a whisper. "It's close to where NASA launches rockets to the moon."

My memory whizzed back to two years before. We didn't own a television set, but in 1969 Dad had rented a small black-and-white television for a very special event. The picture had been fuzzy and kept jumping, but our excited little family had been riveted to the screen. We watched, breathless, as the lunar module set down on the surface and astronaut Neil Armstrong slowly descended and stepped onto the moon.

Many people in Port St. Joe hadn't believed that we, as a nation, had gone to the moon. But I had. I had been captivated by the entire notion that a rocket ship could take humans from Earth to the moon.

Now, we were moving to the Space Coast, close to where they actually launched the rockets. My imagination filled with astronauts and countdowns and blastoffs.

I grinned at Dad. "When do we leave?"

I rode in the moving truck beside Dad. We drove south on Interstate 75 and were inundated with billboards that proclaimed the imminent opening of a new and wonderful place called Walt Disney World. The colorful signs caught my eye, but I peppered Dad with questions about Palm Bay. I couldn't get away from the thought of rockets blasting off to space in my "backyard."

Soon after we arrived in Palm Bay—a small town but alive with potential—Dad found the Indian River, just a half mile from our new church, and all the fishing that it offered. Our first time there, Dad waded out into the river with his cast net. He caught so many mullet fish that he had to stick them in his pockets and belt.

I kept searching the sky for rockets.

Dad looked over at me and chuckled. "You know, in a few weeks we could go over to Cape Canaveral and watch the launch of Apollo 15."

My eyes snapped to Dad's.

As he looked for a pocket to stuff another fish into, he casually added, "This mission is scheduled to take a car along, a lunar roving vehicle. The astronauts are going to drive it on the moon."

"What? You have to be kidding me!" My young mind danced with untethered enthusiasm.

Dad raised a teasing eyebrow at me and said, "What do you think? Do you want to go to the launch?"

On the morning of July 26, 1971, my family waited anxiously by the Indian River with thousands of other people to witness the launch of Apollo 15. A large digital clock counted down the seconds. When finally the one gave way to that glorious, heart-stopping zero, my gaze shifted toward the horizon.

Fire filled the sky. The immense Saturn V rocket rose from the Earth—in silence, it seemed. Then after a brief moment, a powerful roar thundered over us.

We watched the rocket rise and rise, growing higher, growing smaller, reduced to a sliver, then reduced to a speck. It vanished, pulling along a smoke trail that seemed thin as thread.

One day, I decided as I watched that thread, *I will go to the moon.*

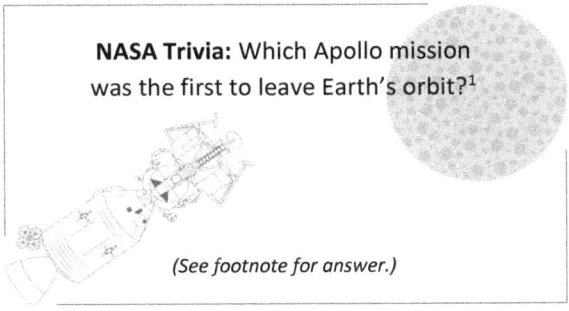

NASA Trivia: Which Apollo mission was the first to leave Earth's orbit?[1]

(See footnote for answer.)

After NASA retired the Saturn V rocket and their trips to the moon subsided, they began to develop the shuttle program. As a high school student, I took every aeronautical class I could while keeping both eyes on the shuttle program just up the road.

---

[1] Apollo 8. The astronauts aboard were Mission Commander Frank Borman, Lunar Module Pilot Bill Anders, and Command Module Pilot Jim Lovell.

Gradually I began to feel God calling me to a mission other than the moon. After high school, I enrolled in seminary and moved away to attend.

The shuttle program continued with unparalleled success. Soon, as a country, we even stopped paying attention to each flight.

Several years passed as I graduated from seminary school and traveled as a youth evangelist before returning to the Space Coast. Back home I assisted my father in the church that he pastored, and I also worked as a reporter at a Christian radio station. To my delight, my boss assigned me to cover the upcoming launch of the space shuttle *Challenger*.

On January 28, 1986, an unusually cold day, I provided commentary on live radio while watching and awaiting the shuttle launch, a direct audio feed from Mission Control in my ear.

As the shuttle lifted off, I announced and described it with a mix of college-graduate professionalism and genuine childlike wonder.

Through the audio feed, I heard the words of Mission Control. "*Challenger*, go at throttle up." I heard Mission Commander Dick Scobee reply, "Roger, go at throttle up."

I tilted my head back as the *Challenger* rose, reporting the sights and sounds. Seconds later, the shuttle blew up in a massive explosion high over my head.

Stunned, I held the microphone, saying nothing.

The Mission Control feed in my ear went silent.

The people around me seemed frozen in time.

Could the crew have survived the explosion? What happened to the crew?

Watching smoky debris trails rain down, I thought back sixteen years to April 1970 when the historic Apollo 13 mission had almost lost its three astronauts in space. Six days had passed while the nation held its collective breath. Astronauts Jim Lovell, Jack

Swigert, and Fred Haise had been considered doomed, due to a series of disasters that repeatedly threatened their lives and prevented them from landing on the moon. I had been unaware of this as a boy. To me, everyone working at NASA was invincible.

Now I wondered, "Why couldn't the *Challenger* have experienced troubles more like those of Apollo 13, where the crew eventually made it home?"

In time I came to understand that the odds-defying, life-saving events that unfolded during the Apollo 13 mission were miraculous. I've also observed that each and every one of us experiences unexpected, and sometimes deeply traumatic, events throughout life that can rock us and throw us off course.

For some, that unexpected event may be the death of a family member or dear friend. For others, it may be the loss of a marriage, confinement to a wheelchair, or an emotional prison. Every precious, human life experiences trials and crises.

Why, in a world with an all-powerful and all-loving God, do such bad things happen? How can we survive these things and right the ship? How do we get back on—and stay on—course and keep trusting God, even though new crises may eventually impact our lives?

The more I studied the crises and divine interventions in the Apollo 13 mission, the more God revealed the answers to those questions. This book presents thirteen little-known touches of God's presence and power that saved the disaster-stricken mission and the lives of its astronauts. Touches that can help each of us, when we face crises, to manage the fire and marshal the miraculous.

For me, the questions hadn't yet come to me when I was a boy, back in April 1970, while Apollo 13 prepared to liftoff. I simply spent my playtime imagining what it would be like to be an astronaut.

Apollo 13 was launched at 13:13 CST (Mission Control time) on April 11, 1970. . . .

Apollo 13 crew: Jim Lovell, Jack Swigert and Fred Haise. Credit: NASA

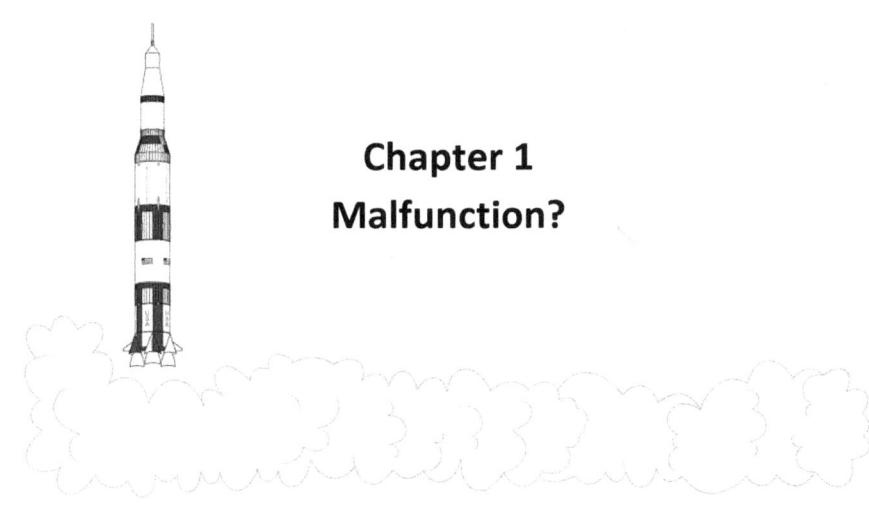

Chapter 1
Malfunction?

Apollo 13 Miracle #1: Center Engine Cutoff

Just five minutes thirty seconds after the launch of Apollo 13, during the second-stage boost, the center ("inboard") engine, engine number five, cut off. In the command module, its warning light switched on, startling astronauts Jim Lovell, Jack Swigert, and Fred Haise. They communicated with Mission Control in Houston, Texas.

Swigert: "Inboard."

CapCom (Mission Control): "We confirm inboard out."

Lovell: "That shouldn't have happened."

Swigert: "No, that's [scheduled for] 7:42 [minutes]. That's two minutes early."

Uneasiness fell over Mission Control and the crew. Then Mission Control determined the four remaining engines would be able to compensate by operating for four additional minutes.

Everyone on the spacecraft breathed a sigh of relief. Mission Commander Jim Lovell said to the other two, "Hey, that's our crisis." The astronauts figured their trouble was over and the remaining flight would be smooth.

All in all, the shutdown wasn't really a problem.

But, had the center engine not mysteriously shut down, a catastrophic failure would have ensued.

NASA's warning system engineer Jerry Woodfill was a member of the team of experts who manned the Mission Evaluation Room (MER) at Johnson Space Center in Houston during the mission. He said, "What happened was the Saturn V rocket experienced dangerous so-called 'pogo' thrust oscillations, a problem NASA knew about."

A fix was scheduled to be implemented . . . for Apollo 14.

"The oscillations are like a jackhammer, and it was so dreadful on Apollo 6 that it tore off a panel on the booster and threatened the mission," Woodfill said. "However, Apollo 13 was a much different situation than Apollo 6.

"The Apollo 6 mission carried a mock lunar lander of more modest mass than the 'full-up' lander which Apollo 13 carried to orbit. With the added mass for Apollo 13, the pogo forces were suddenly a magnitude greater in intensity. A mission report said that the engine experienced 68g vibrations at 16 hertz, flexing the thrust frame by 3 inches (76 mm).

"If the center engine had continued running a few more seconds, the oscillations may have destroyed the vehicle. That engine was pounding horizontally up and down, a quarter foot, at the rate of 16 times a second," Woodfill said. "The engine had become a two-ton sledgehammer, a deadly pogo stick of destruction, putting enormous forces on the supporting structures."

So, what shut the center engine down?

Woodfill said, "It is, to this day, not fully understood, but it had something to do with fooling the engine's thrust chamber pressure sensor that pressure was too low.

"Though the shutdown command came from a low thrust chamber pressure sensor assessment, actually the engine was operating correctly," he said. "The sensor had nothing to do with the pogo phenomenon. For some inexplicable reason, it was like something sucked the pressure out of the chamber and a sensor turned the engine off. But no one knows exactly why.

"Something intervened, stopping the engine from pounding its way from the mount into the fragile fuel tanks. This would have destroyed the Apollo 13 launch vehicle."

Malfunction, or God-function?

What appears to be a mistake, mishap, or trouble may actually be the hand of God. In the Old Testament, Joseph knew this as well as anyone.

As a young man, Joseph was sold into slavery by his brothers, who then told their father that he had been killed.

Joseph was purchased as a slave by Potiphar, Pharaoh's captain of the guard. Potiphar, a leader of men, saw Joseph's leadership potential and promoted him to head of his household. There Joseph gained leadership experience. But when Potiphar's wife made advances toward Joseph, Joseph refused her, and she falsely accused Joseph of rape. Joseph was thrown into prison.

His warden soon saw him as a leader of men, and placed Joseph in charge of everyone in the prison. Joseph gained more leadership experience, over more people, for many years. Later, Pharaoh's butler fell out of good graces with the king, and found himself in prison with Joseph. Eventually the butler was restored to the palace. But rather than remember to help Joseph who was in prison unjustly, the butler forgot him.

Only when no one could interpret the dream of Pharaoh did the butler finally remember Joseph. Then Joseph was called out of prison to interpret the dream of Pharaoh. After he did, he was promoted to what was essentially vice president of Egypt, in charge of food distribution during the world-wide famine. His years of leadership experience enabled him to lead the world.

Malfunctions, or God-functions? Clearly God was at work through the events that took place. Joseph realized this. During the famine his brothers came to him to request food, not knowing the man they spoke to was their brother.

"Then Joseph said to his brothers, 'Come close to me.' When they had done so, he said, 'I am your brother Joseph, the one you sold into Egypt! And now, do not be distressed and do not be angry with yourselves for selling me here, because it was to save lives that God sent me ahead of you. For two years now there has been famine in the land, and for the next five years there will not be plowing and reaping. But God sent me ahead of you to preserve for you a remnant on earth and to save your lives by a great deliverance.

So then, it was not you who sent me here, but God. He made me father to Pharaoh, lord of his entire household and ruler of all Egypt'" (Genesis 45:4-8).

Joseph essentially told his brothers, "I have been tested. I've been through it for a reason. The reason was that I would not just be saved, but that I could save others. God brought me to this place. He let things shut down in my life to get me to this place. It was unexplainable at the time, but now I can see the hand of God in every situation." Not a malfunction, but a God-function. Knowing that, Joseph found purpose in his pain. He found a blessing in the betrayal.

From Pain to Promise

Joseph's mind-set is revealed in the priorities of his questions and statements to his brothers.

Hope is where Joseph starts. *"'I am Joseph! Is my father still living?'" (Genesis 45:3b).* Joseph chose to live not in the pain of the past but the hope of the present.

How many times do we miss the present by living in the past or in the future? Nothing is more important than the present, because you can do something about the present. You can't change the past, and the future isn't here yet, but the present is here now. Here we have hope.

Hurt is revealed in the next statement. *"'I am your brother Joseph, the one you sold into Egypt!'" (Genesis 45:4).* Joseph remembered the betrayal of his brothers and was reminding them. The incident wasn't being swept under the rug. He never forgot it, but he didn't let it define him.

Healing is shown in the next verse. *"'And now, do not be distressed and do not be angry with yourselves for selling me here, because it was to save lives that God sent me ahead of you'" (Genesis 45:5).*

God doesn't expect us to forget the pain of our past. He just expects us to focus on the promise of today. In many ways He takes us from the darkness of pain to the light of His promises.

Hurt

Like Joseph, sometimes we are hurt by rejection or a loss. God never wastes a hurt. God may be preparing us for something greater.

While I was in South Africa a few weeks ago, three men in a car pretended to be police and pulled us over. I was a passenger in the car driven by a missionary who has lived in that area for fifteen years.

These three men worked us over for the next twenty minutes, searching us, our wallets, and the car. All the time they pretended to be police. They ended up stealing only from me—$100 from my wallet and a fake Rolex watch that was worth about $25.

The interesting aspect of this was that just before I left home for Africa, my nice Tag Heuer watch that our church had given to me for my tenth pastoral anniversary was put in the shop for battery repair. I always wear this watch because it's waterproof and has sentimental value to me. When the battery dies, the watch is sent back to Switzerland for a new battery and then the watch is resealed. While it's being repaired, I wear some cheap backup watch. The Lord had preserved my special watch for me ahead of time, but I had seen it as a loss. I didn't realize that sometimes things are taken from you to preserve them.

What I'd thought had been a watch malfunction had actually been a God-function. He preserved me from the hurt of losing a cherished gift.

Death, which we see as the worst kind of hurt, is a way that God preserves people. We see it as a loss, but God takes someone close to us and secures them for eternity.

Helplessness

Sometimes we are put in situations that make us totally dependent on God. The trouble comes not to cause us discomfort, but to develop our faith in God. He wants us to trust Him.

I felt impressed in our church to launch a debt-reduction campaign in the middle of the economic recession when many of the families in our congregation were in foreclosure on their homes. My leaders and advisors all said that the timing wasn't good, but God kept pushing me by telling me, "Do it now, so that I will get glory from it."

We did it, and God worked one miracle after another. People began to sacrifice, and the church started shedding their debt day by day. In addition, people began to get their homes and jobs back. It was a faith builder for our entire church.

God wants us to depend on Him. Sometimes we are put into a position of helplessness so that we stay close to God and dependent on Him, as Joseph was.

Preparation

How many times has something broken in our lives and we thought it meant the absence of God? A broken job. A broken relationship. A broken body.

I'm sure something has broken at one point in your life; few get through adulthood without experiencing this. Something or someone in your life . . . just shut down. Then you cried through the night, overwhelmed with grief, questioning God and trying to find a reasonable, rational answer, if he's even there. He seems so distant.

Little did you know, God was preparing you so that you would be able to cope with something greater, so that you would be able to endure. He may have even prepared you so that you could save your own or someone else's life.

When I page through the Old Testament, I imagine David as a shepherd boy trying to figure out why wild animals—a bear one time, another time a lion—attacked him and his sheep. He was able to defeat the predators, but he likely wondered, "Why did they come after me? None of the other shepherds have been attacked."

Sometime later, when David heard the giant, Goliath, roar on the battlefield against God's army, David understood why he'd had to fight a bear and a lion. He knew why God had allowed the attacks. God had been preparing him for a greater challenge.

"He trains my hands for battle; my arms can bend a bow of bronze" (Psalm 18:34).

Through troubles, God prepared Joseph and David. Likewise He uses troubles to prepare us for greater challenges, and greater achievements.

Strengthening

When he killed Goliath, David must have thought his trouble was over, but it was only starting. Gradually David learned, "The same God who helped me with a bear, helped me with a lion. The same God who helped me with a bear and a lion, helped me with a giant. The same God who helped me with a giant, helped me with King Saul, and in hiding, and in battle. The same God who did all these things will help me with my rebellious son Absalom, who is trying to kill me and take the throne."

That knowledge strengthened David's faith. It enabled him to increasingly trust God.

Moses may have thought his trouble was over when Aaron's snake ate all the snakes of the magicians in Pharaoh's court (Exodus 7:12). That was just the beginning of his trouble. The demands Moses and Aaron made of Pharaoh were met with even harsher restrictions and punishment on the Hebrews. The Hebrew people likely thought Moses' talk of deliverance did nothing except make their work harder.

Gradually, God's powerful interventions strengthened the faith of Moses, Aaron, and the Hebrew people. The confrontations with Pharaoh advanced their trust in God.

You can think back over your life and lament your failures and troubles, or you can observe how through each one God may have brought you greater strength, increased faith, and more resilient trust in Him.

As Moses realized while standing before Pharaoh, there would be ups and downs, but with every disappointment would come deliverance. God had been strengthening him—and Joseph and David and others—so they would be ready for many challenges ahead.

"He gives strength to the weary and increases
the power of the weak.
Even youths grow tired and weary,
and young men stumble and fall;
but those who hope in the Lord will renew their strength.

They will soar on wings like eagles;
they will run and not grow weary,
they will walk and not be faint" (Isaiah 40:29-31).

"*Consider it pure joy, my brothers, whenever you face trials of many kinds, because you know that the testing of your faith develops perseverance. Perseverance must finish its work so that you may be mature and complete, not lacking anything*" (James 1:2-4).

God doesn't change with time. As He did with Joseph, David, and Moses, He still uses "malfunctions" to strengthen us today. And to take us from pain to promise.

> **NASA Trivia:** Which Apollo mission crew is listed in Guinness World Records for flying the farthest from Earth?[2]
>
> *(See footnote for answer.)*

Prayer

Imagine: Just five minutes thirty seconds after launch, during the second-stage boost, the center engine, engine number five, cuts off. In the command module, its warning light switches on.

You're an astronaut strapped on top a malfunctioning rocket hurling into space. What do you do?

"'Call upon Me in the day of trouble;
I will deliver you, and you will honor Me'" (Psalm 50:15).

---

[2] The crew of Apollo 13. Their above-Earth altitude reached 248,655 miles while they flew their partial orbit around the moon.

God wants an ongoing relationship with each one of us. If it's been a while since we've chatted with God in prayer, He has a knack for getting our attention. Specifically—problems, dilemmas, catastrophes.

Yes, those may come even when we maintain a consistent and heartfelt prayer life. But if we don't and trouble erupts, it may be God seeking and knocking, reminding us he's close by and waiting for us to ask Him for help.

> *"The Lord is near to all who call on Him,*
> *to all who call on Him in truth.*
> *He fulfills the desires of those who fear Him;*
> *He hears their cry and saves them" (Psalm 145:18-19).*

"Jesus told His disciples a parable to show them that they should always pray and not give up" (Luke 18:1).

God often takes us from pain to promise through prayer.

Patience and Wisdom

Sometimes there is a long gap of time between the trial and the triumph. Between the "malfunction" and the miraculous. The miraculous is not always expedient.

Ultimately, each of us in our own journey come to crossroads, decisions that will shape our future and our destiny. We face the temptation of the fast track. We find ourselves looking for the quick fix. Yet in our hearts we know that God orders the steps of righteous people.

> *"In his heart a man plans his course,*
> *but the Lord determines his steps" (Proverbs 16:9).*

Steps, not strides. Sometimes it is just one small step for us but a giant leap for what God is doing. Through pain, God can develop our patience.

During the Apollo 11 mission, five minutes into Neil Armstrong and Buzz Aldrin's descent in the lunar module and 6000 feet above the surface of the moon, their onboard computer systems set off program alarms. They contemplated aborting the landing while 600 million people around the globe held their breath.

Mission Control told the astronauts that it was safe to continue their descent. Apparently, the program alarms indicated "executive overflows," meaning the guidance computer could not complete all its tasks in real time and had to postpone some of them. The alarms were programed in the software to inform the astronauts of this prioritizing maneuver. Engineers and software designers had had enough foresight to write the software so that it could think on its own and prioritize the tasks it was being asked to do. It recognized what was most important at the moment, what had to be postponed, and then signaled the astronauts of this decision.

Our lives have to function the same way. Sometimes we only have seconds to respond, but we must be able to focus on what is crucial and ignore what is not necessary. If we try to do too much, we crash.

Emotionally, many people get so many signals they can't keep the main thing the main thing. On the other hand, unexpected troubles may paralyze us. Stop us in our tracks. At such times, ask God for patience and wisdom, calm and clarity.

"He stilled the storm to a whisper;
the waves of the sea were hushed.
They were glad when it grew calm,
and He guided them to their desired haven" (Psalm 107:29-30).

With the patience and wisdom we gain, God can take us from pain to promise.

It should also be noted that it's important for each of us to learn the valuable lesson of moving on to some other task when we are stuck in a crisis. Joseph didn't sit in Potiphar's house and do nothing. Nor did he sit in prison and do nothing. He patiently, wisely trusted God, and pressed on.

Opportunity

In our humanity, we cannot presume to know every reason why God does what He does, but knowing all of the above may help lead us through dark days.

Pain is a tool. Disappointment is an opportunity.

The things that you and I see as failures and problems ("malfunctions"), God uses for progress. The circumstances that you and I fret over, God uses to fortify our spirits. The measure of our spiritual advancement is not confined to the struggles and stumbles; it is the strength of setbacks that ultimately defines our success.

Many times we survive a test and think we're back to where we started. We don't see that what we thought was a broken attempt to accomplish was actually a training session for our future.

Each failure can blow you off course, or it can fuel your next success. God uses the fuel of failure to propel us to our promises. Malfunctions are often God-functions.

On board the spacecraft, the center engine, engine number five, shut down. Though they didn't realize it at the time, this shutdown was more of a miracle than a mishap. The inexplicable malfunction, which at first the astronauts believed to be a significant failure, was actually a God-function, one that carried them from the pain of mission failure to the promise of greater things to come.

But this was only the beginning of the malfunctions they would face, and the miracles God would provide.

Almost certainly, this malfunction saved the spacecraft and the men.

Apollo 13, miracle number one.

FAITH ACCELERATOR

Take a few minutes and write down disappointments or unexpected circumstances ("malfunctions") that happened in your life that prepared you to overcome greater challenges.

In other words, list the disappointments or unexpected circumstances God allowed to happen. After each entry, list the benefits that resulted from the difficult situation. The benefits might or might not include greater faith.

This and upcoming Faith Accelerators will be here for you to review for years to come whenever your faith needs a rocket boost.

_____
_____
_____
_____
_____
_____
_____
_____
_____
_____
_____
_____
_____
_____
_____
_____
_____
_____
_____
_____
_____

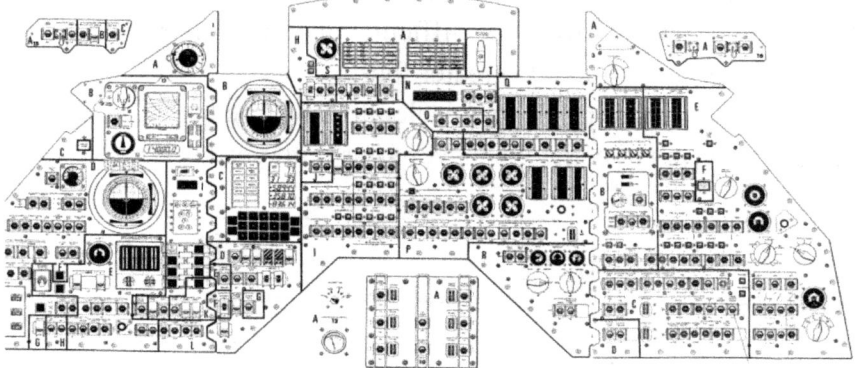

Diagram of the Apollo command module main control panel.
Oxygen quantity gauges are located near the top right of the panel.
Credit: NASA History Office.

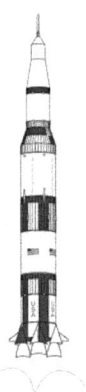

Chapter 2
The Value of Imperfection

Apollo 13 Miracle #2: A Faulty Gauge
April 13, 1970, 9:05 p.m.

Six minutes after the Apollo 13 crew finished their TV broadcast that highlighted the pleasure and relative comfort of working in a weightless environment, Mission Control communicated with Jack Swigert.

CapCom: "13, we've got one more item for you, when you get a chance. We'd like you to stir up your cryo tanks."

Swigert: "Okay. Stand by."

At the control panel, Swigert reached out his hand to perform the requested cryo-stir.

Oxygen tank one's fans switched on. Normal operation followed.

Oxygen tank two's fans switched on. An electrical short was indicated.

Warning lights began to flash on. Tank two's pressure began to rise.

An Apollo crew's oxygen tanks were typically stirred once every twenty-four hours. Since the cryogenic oxygen in the tanks tended to solidify, a crew routinely performed stirs so they could get a near-accurate reading of O2 level on the gauge.

However, though Apollo 13 was just under 56 hours into its mission, this was the fifth stir of the oxygen tanks, averaging one stir every eleven hours. Why so many stirs?

The quantity gauge had been malfunctioning on O2 tank two.

As a means to troubleshoot the faulty gauge, Mission Control had asked the astronauts to more frequently actuate the stirrer.

Due to the faulty oxygen gauge, the explosion that was about to follow this stir happened in a way that the astronauts could survive. Had the gauge been functioning properly, the fifth stir that was about to result in an explosion would have happened a few days later, while Lovell and Haise were on the moon and Swigert was alone in the spacecraft. Swigert would have been thrown off course, unable to return for Lovell and Haise, or return to Earth. All three astronauts would have perished.

The Imperfect Human Need for Order amid Chaos

Mission Control asked the astronauts to stir the oxygen tanks in order to figure out the problem with the gauge. It is our nature to try to bring about order amid chaos. We strive to find some semblance of normalcy in an effort to deal with an unexpected turn of events. Sometimes this need sidetracks us while we're searching for order, making it an imperfect human need.

After Judas betrayed Jesus and took his own life, Acts 1 reveals that Jesus' disciples got together and decided, "We need to fill this open spot and select another disciple, with the Lord directing us."

Chaos had followed Judas's betrayal of Jesus. Judas had been one of the twelve disciples. He had been part of the inner circle. This unexpected turn of events quickly led to the crucifixion of Jesus by the Romans. The gospels of the New Testament record that Jesus was resurrected following the crucifixion, proving Himself to those who believed and to some who doubted.

The Bible then reveals that Jesus ascended back into heaven from Mt. Olivet (the Mount of Olives) while His disciples stood around looking into heaven. This scene reminds me of January 28, 1986 when we all stood around for hours looking at the lingering smoke from the Space Shuttle *Challenger* explosion on the shore of the Atlantic Ocean.

All of those events in the later part of the gospels and in Acts 1 led the apostles to feel compelled to restore order. "We need to handle some church business. We have an unresolved matter." This is common to humanity.

The disciples and followers of Jesus gathered in the upper room, a meeting place in Jerusalem following the ascension of Christ. The believers of Christ were perhaps praying when the apostle Peter stood up and said, "We need to take care of a matter."

Peter proceeded to describe what happened to Judas in gory detail. This must have stopped the prayer meeting immediately. Peter then gave us a hint to the compulsion they were feeling to make this matter right. He said, *"He (Judas) was one of our number and shared in this ministry" (Acts 1:17).*

Judas was numbered with us. Judas had obtained a part of this ministry. There is a hole now. There is a missing piece of the puzzle.

Those missing pieces drive us crazy in our imperfect humanity.

Have you ever lost a piece of the puzzle? Our obsessive-compulsive nature as humans will cause us to lose sleep over a lack of completeness. A missing piece. A missing part. An empty blank. We need things to fit. Our humanity needs this type of order.

The followers of Jesus were supposed to be seeking the Holy Spirit, as Jesus had commanded. They would do so in the next chapter, but right now they had this nagging issue of missing a disciple. They had a hard time praying while there was unresolved business.

The criterion that Jesus' disciples established for this selection process was only that the candidate be a witness of His resurrection. That was pretty broad. As Paul recorded in 1 Corinthians 15:6, *"After that, He appeared to more than five hundred of the brothers at the same time."* The process quickly narrowed as they chose two men, Joseph called Barsabbas, who was surnamed Justus, and Matthias.

They cast lots, which was their custom, believing that God would orchestrate the results. They prayed and asked God to direct the outcome. Acts 1 reveals that Matthias was chosen. Acts 1:26 simply says, *"Then they cast lots, and the lot fell to Matthias; so he was [numbered with] the eleven apostles."*

Twice the Bible mentions this phrase with this process. Judas was numbered, and now Matthias is numbered. As he wrote the book of Acts, Luke was careful to mention this detail to give us insight to how important it was for the apostles to have this number thing complete. Restored. Fixed. Oh thank the Lord, we can get back to the prayer meeting now! We will be able to focus now.

The Holy Spirit was poured out in the very beginning of the next chapter. Three thousand people were added to the church that day, history for mankind was forever changed for the next two thousand plus years, but Matthias was never mentioned again in the Bible.

Apparently, God had a different plan. Man wanted this vacancy filled. Man wanted the congruency of being whole again. That box was checked. That matter was resolved. We once again have twelve apostles. Order is restored. Everything fits. We can move on now.

God gave them this, but then God blew the whole thing up by selecting Saul in Acts 9 and changing his name to Paul. God didn't need a selection committee to choose Paul. He just knocked him off his horse with a bright light. Blinded him. "Paul, what are you doing! You're working against Me!"

When the apostles were casting lots a few chapters earlier, they prayed and said, "God you know the hearts of men." God must have been thinking, "Yes, I do, and why have you only given Me two to choose from?" God does not respond to the box that man tries to put Him in. Instead of the disciples being whole again with twelve apostles, they now had thirteen, and the one God picked was having an unprecedented revival.

Paul encapsulated this process in his writing to the church in Corinth.

"Last of all He appeared to me also, as to one abnormally born. For I am the least of the apostles and do not even deserve to be called an apostle, because I persecuted the church of God. But by the grace of God I am what I am" (1 Corinthians 15:8-10a).

You can have a plan and God will blow it up. You can make a mold and God will break it. He broke it with Paul. He broke it with Jacob. He broke it with David, a shepherd whom God selected to be king.

Throughout all of the Word of God, we see how God works in accomplishing His will. Oftentimes it is counterintuitive to man's reasoning. Twelve just fits. Twelve apostles. Twelve baskets left over. Twelve foundations of heaven. Twelve is all over the Bible. It's the number of completeness.

But what about the number thirteen? Apollo 13 launched at 13:13 CST (Mission Control time), on April 13, 1970. Thirteen is a number we run from. People don't like the number. Have you ever noticed in an elevator, there is no thirteenth button, even though there may be twenty stories? How did they build a tall building and leave out the thirteenth floor?

There is no thirteenth row in an airplane. I mean, thirteen does not even get invited to the party. There obviously is a thirteenth floor in a tall building and a thirteenth row on an airplane. They just do not get labeled as thirteen. The builders go from twelve to fourteen. Just skip it. Why? Because people will not sit in the thirteenth row on an airplane.

People will not stay on the thirteenth floor in a hotel. They request a change. They tell the front desk, "I need another room on a different floor. I can't handle this thirteenth floor. I can't sleep. I have a bad feeling about this. I don't like thirteen. It makes me uncomfortable."

Our culture has put a label on thirteen that it is "unlucky." Thirteen cannot seem to break this stigma. That's because we are imperfect humans.

Many people had an apprehension about thirteen prior to the launch of Apollo 13.

But its three astronauts who rocketed toward space wouldn't need skeptics talking about how unlucky thirteen is. They would need people to help them who didn't subscribe to conspiracy theories. They would need engineers who could break the mold, engage in unconventional thinking, and figure out how to solve the problem.

The faulty gauge would be the least of their challenges. They, like we, would need order amid the chaos. But how does a perfect God deal with our human imperfection?

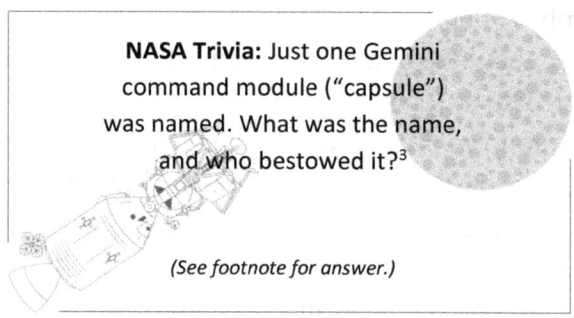

NASA Trivia: Just one Gemini command module ("capsule") was named. What was the name, and who bestowed it?[3]

(See footnote for answer.)

---

[3] The command module of Gemini 3 was *Molly Brown* ("the Unsinkable"), humorously bestowed by astronaut Gus Grissom who nearly drowned when his previous capsule, *Liberty Bell 7*, sank shortly after splashing down in the Atlantic Ocean. (The sinking of *Liberty Bell 7* led to the addition of inflatable flotation collars to subsequent capsules.)

God Uses Imperfection

Though some might consider it mere irony, I believe God likes to work against the grain of our grand ideas. God swims upstream when everyone else swims downstream. We like people, processes, and instruments to function predictably, but God likes to use the imperfect to do the impossible.

The miraculous was never supposed to be proper. It was never in the nature of God to confine His power to our preconceptions.

Can God really use *us* to make a positive difference in the world? Can He truly use erring, fallible, imperfect us? The Bible reveals God's answer.

He used children, cowards, the physically impaired, fishermen, tax collectors, and more, plus an executioner of preachers whom God turned into an apostle.

And God used a faulty oxygen quantity gauge to save the Apollo 13 astronauts.

In 1 Samuel 16, God told His prophet Samuel to anoint as king the son of Jesse that God would reveal. When Samuel met Jesse, Jesse gave Samuel a lineup of his sons to pick from, those sons Jesse thought were worthy candidates to be king. What he considered worthy did not include David. David was the youngest brother, who was out back with the sheep and a harp, writing poems and telling wild stories of killing bears and lions. Maybe his father thought, "David has an overactive imagination. I'd better not invite him to this visit with Samuel. He may embarrass us."

I love the way God works! He always picks people we would never pick.

Samuel prayed for each son of Jesse, but the Lord said, *No.* Next one. *No.* Next one. *No.*

Finally, Samuel asked, "Are there any more sons?"

Jesse basically answered, "Well, yes . . . there is this little, ruddy one who's out in the field with the sheep."

Samuel said, "Send for him." Samuel already knew this was the next king. He didn't even need to see him. He knew how God works. The Word of God provides multiple examples of how God does the unexpected in accomplishing His will. Often His actions are counterintuitive to man's reasoning.

God uses imperfection.

Many of us today need a God who, when everybody else says, "He'll never amount to anything," looks beyond our faults and says, "He may be unconventional, but I can use him." We need a God who says, "His parents may have been alcoholics, but I can save him." "She may have made a lot of mistakes, society may have given up on her, but I have a plan for her life."

"If we confess our sins, He is faithful and just and will forgive us our sins and purify us from all unrighteousness" (1 John 1:9).

The glory of God is never clearer than when He loves the unlovable and saves the unsavable. You need not worry if you have nothing to offer God. He paints on a blank canvas. You need not worry if you have no talent. He is the giver of every good gift. You need not worry if you have a history void of spiritual pursuit. He can create a wellspring in a desert. You do not have to be emotionally fit to find spiritual faith.

The power of God is never limited by man's problems. Not only can God work around me to accomplish His will, but He works through me to accomplish His will and receives glory for using a flawed human.

"God was pleased through the foolishness of what was preached to save those who believe" (1 Corinthians 1:21b).

"Faith comes from hearing the message, and the message is heard through the word of Christ" (Romans 10:17).

God used Peter to preach to Cornelius in Acts 10. God could have just sent an angel, but instead He used a flawed man. He used Mary as the mother of Jesus, and many others in similar ways.

Don't let your own mind or your own emotions talk you out of what God is wanting to do with your life. God uses imperfection.

God doesn't care who we were. He cares who we are. No matter how imperfect we've been, God saved us anyhow. He not only gave us a miracle through Jesus' death and resurrection, it was an improper miracle. It did not make sense. It did not fit. There was no order to it. There was no precedent for it.

How do you explain God picking an executioner who was killing preachers to be the next apostle? Every law and every logical thought would revolt against such an idea.

God chose Jacob for the birthright though Esau was the oldest.

How do you explain the timeline of Gentile salvation being disrupted with a little lady, part Syrian and part Phoenician, convincing Jesus to open the doors ahead of time with her hunger and humility?

The disciples eating corn on the Sabbath!

The lame man in Acts 3!

The paralyzed servant in Matthew 8!

The five loaves and two fishes feeding a multitude of thousands!

If you were to study each of these miracles carefully, you would find that some archaic custom or logical explanation was missing, but God is God.

You can't deny what God is doing. You can't stop it. You can't box it. You can't minimize it with traditions and laws.

God challenges our thinking with the unexplainable and the unexpected. Everything is on the table with God, even the things we have taken off the table with our fears and misconceptions.

"Now to Him who is able to do immeasurably more than all we ask or imagine, according to His power that is at work within us..." (Ephesians 3:20).

God is a God of improper miracles.

*"'For My thoughts are not your thoughts,
neither are your ways My ways,'
declares the Lord.
'As the heavens are higher than the earth,
so are My ways higher than your ways
and My thoughts than your thoughts'"* (Isaiah 55:8-9).

The flaws in our flesh that would disqualify us in our own minds are a tool in the hand of God to create something beautiful. God doesn't need anything already developed to work with. He is Creator and can do great works in spite of our flaws.

God uses imperfection through us on Earth, just as He used a faulty oxygen gauge aboard a spacecraft on its way to the moon. A faulty gauge which required more frequent stirs of the oxygen tanks, and so ensured that the explosion that was about to happen would do so in a way the astronauts could survive.

Apollo 13, miracle number two.

FAITH ACCELERATOR

List times when God used you to positively influence the faith life of someone else, whether in major ways or minor, despite your imperfections.

After each entry, note what you said or did that proved effective, or what you might say or do differently if you encounter a similar situation. Having this foreknowledge empowers you. Pray for inspired ideas and for a passion to use them.

Continue to keep a log of ways that you positively influence faith in others, and note fresh ideas for communicating God's presence, love, and salvation as He inspires them in you.

Remind yourself often that God uses imperfection.

_____
_____
_____
_____
_____
_____
_____
_____
_____
_____
_____
_____
_____
_____
_____
_____
_____
_____
_____
_____
_____
_____
_____
_____
_____
_____
_____

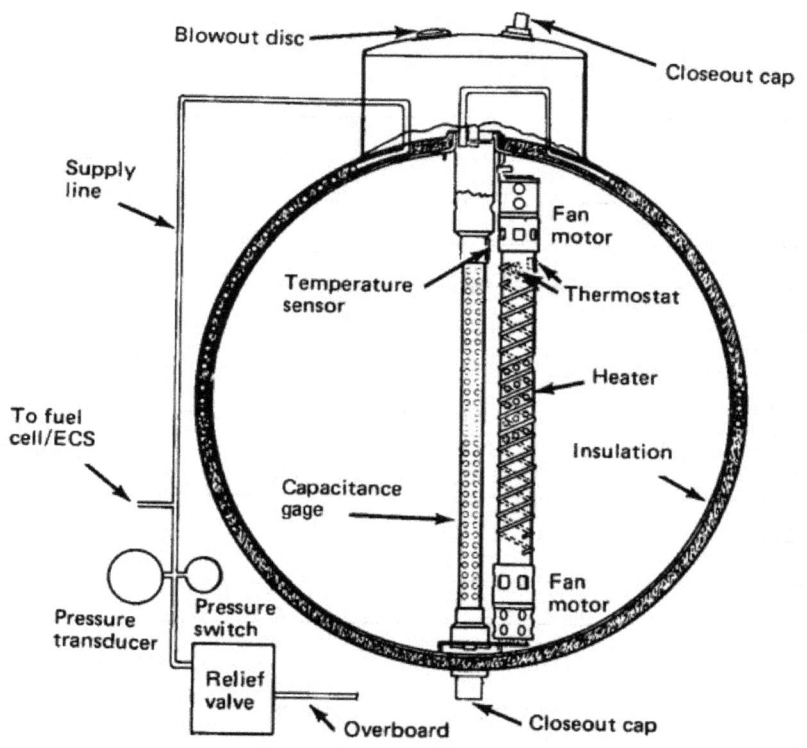

*Internal diagram of an Apollo oxygen tank.
Credit: NASA.*

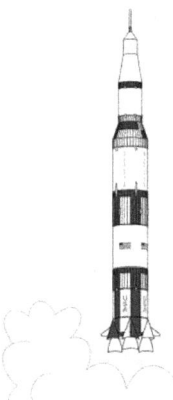

Chapter 3
All in God's Time

Apollo 13 Miracle #3: Timing
April 13, 1970, 9:08 p.m.

An explosion—***BANG!***—jolted the astronauts. A large thirteen-foot high panel was blown off the exterior of the service module beside oxygen tank two.

Inside the command module, the telemetry went down for 1.8 seconds. When function resumed, the O2 tank two quantity gauge read off-the-scale high, suggesting a sensor failure.

Swigert: "Okay, Houston, we've had a problem here."

CapCom: "This is Houston. Say again, please."

Lovell: "Houston, we've had a problem. We've had a main B bus undervolt."

CapCom: "Roger. Main B bus undervolt. . . ."

For fifty-nine seconds, the temperature in O2 tank two descended in a steady drop, further suggesting a sensor failure.

Haise: "Okay. Right now, Houston, the voltage is - is looking good. And we had a pretty large bang associated with the caution and warning there. And as I recall, main B was the one that had an amp spike on it once before."

CapCom: "Roger, Fred."

The quantity readout of O2 tank two was erratic for more than a minute. Finally the dial settled at off-the-scale low.

The DC main bus B undervoltage triggered the master alarm. Seconds later the alarm was shut off. Through a window of the command module, Lovell noticed a trail of vapor. He communicated with Mission Control in Houston.

Lovell: "It looks to me, looking out the hatch, that we are venting something. We are venting something out into the - into space."

It was their life-giving oxygen, bleeding from O2 tank two.

Why did this have to happen now?

The Original Mission Plan

Lunar Module Pilot Fred Haise and Commander Jim Lovell's assignment was to set the lunar lander *Aquarius* down in the Fra Mauro area and conduct NASA's third moon-surface mission. In addition to collecting rock samples and taking photographs, Lovell and Haise were scheduled to conduct experiments and also sleep eight hours in the lunar module (LM) on the moon. The explosion near the command module (CM) *Odyssey* significantly altered this mission plan.

The second miracle that took place—that the oxygen tank had a faulty sensor which prompted more frequent cryo-stirs—is closely linked to the third incident of divine involvement: the *timing* of the explosion. Had the quantity gauge not been faulty, the fifth twenty-four-hour actuation that caused the electrical short would have occurred aboard the spacecraft a few days later than it did, while Lovell and Haise were down on the lunar surface. Swigert would have been orbiting the moon alone, unable to singlehandedly deal with the life-threatening explosion. He would have been thrown far off course, unable to recover, and Lovell and Haise would never have been able to rejoin Swigert or return to Earth.

God's Strategic Timing

One of the aspects about the nature of God that is often overlooked is that God is the master of timing. Frequently we miss what God wants us to do in our lives because we're frustrated with the *when*.

We've all experienced sudden, intrusive life events that instantly changed our plans. Most of us have even exclaimed, "It couldn't have happened at a worse time!" Likely that was the thought of the astronauts and of everyone at Mission Control. "Why couldn't this explosion have happened shortly after liftoff when a direct-abort burn could have quickly gotten the crew home?"

We think God isn't moving fast enough, or he's moving faster than we want to go. Usually we're ahead of God because we're human and know we have a clock ticking. We tend to rush things, and yet God knows when we are ready and when the timing is right.

Timing is important to the success of most events, but when it comes to spiritual pursuits, perhaps few things are as important as timing. Let's have a look at it from a Biblical viewpoint.

In 1 Corinthians 15, Paul says he was born out of due season. But was he not in the perfect season to bring the gospel to the Gentiles?

In Acts 1 the disciples were not only struggling with the loss of a fellow believer, Judas, they were also struggling with the timing of God's plan.

"So when they met together, they asked Him, 'Lord, are You at this time going to restore the kingdom to Israel?'

He said to them: 'It is not for you to know the times or dates the Father has set by His own authority. But you will receive power when the Holy Spirit comes on you; and you will be My witnesses in Jerusalem, and in all Judea and Samaria, and to the ends of the earth.'

After He said this, He was taken up before their very eyes, and a cloud hid Him from their sight" (Acts 1:6-9).

Jacob didn't understand the timing of having to work seven more years for a father-in-law he didn't trust.

God uses people ahead of their time, like an eight-year-old boy named Josiah to be king of Israel, or people past their prime, like Abraham who was over one hundred years old—and still childless—to be the father of the Jews.

Here are a few principles to consider while you ponder God's timing.

1. God's timing is often disguised as a setback. The most pertinent example: In the Apollo 13 mission, examination of the data after the fact revealed not only how the explosion happened but also just how fortuitous the timing of the explosion had been.

2. We feel the need for speed. Rarely does God. There is no record in the Bible of Jesus ever running. He never got in a hurry. Even when it appeared that He was late because of the pressing needs of the people, He was still right on time. His tardiness in getting to Lazarus, who was very ill in Bethany, ended up with a death and a resurrection (John 11), a miracle that set in motion the events that led to the crucifixion and resurrection of Jesus.

Most of the times that I move outside of God's will is when I want God to do something faster than it's happening, so I try to speed it up. I try to help God with His plan. I try to move it along a little quicker. Somehow, we think God needs us to hurry Him up and get Him moving. Could it be that the right passage for us to get back on track after catastrophes in our lives is to take the longer route?

More than once the Bible says, paraphrased, "Stand still and see the salvation of God" (Exodus 14:13, 2 Chronicles 20:17). But it never says, "Hurry up and see the salvation of God."

"Be still, and know that I am God" (Psalm 46:10a).

The nature of humanity is to work toward reward and away from pain. It's also our nature to work toward reward and away from pain *quickly*. If we suffer an unexpected setback in our lives, our immediate reaction is to try to find the shortest route back to our comfort zones. Often, we end up repeating the same mistake or subjecting ourselves to an even more uncomfortable situation that further threatens our spiritual condition or cripples our faith.

Abraham got into trouble because he tried to hurry God's promise. He and his wife were old and didn't have any children. He figured that he needed to help God with the promise God had given him. So he took Hagar, his wife's handmaid, and they had a son named Ismael. Ismael became the father of the Arabs. Later God revealed to Abraham, "No, that was not My plan."

Eventually Isaac was born of Abraham and Sarah, per God's promise, and plan, *and* timing. Abraham became father of the Jews, by the promise of God, and the father of the Arabs, by man's hurry-it-up plan. They have been at war ever since.

This is another reason why, after Jesus' ascension into heaven, His disciples got in trouble trying to jump the gun with the disciples lot-casting to get Judas's position filled. It is not for us to know the times or the seasons, which the Father has set in His authority (Acts 1:6-8).

Our plans and God's will often clash because of our impatience.

When I was a boy, I was always impatient. I wanted to complete a chore as soon as possible. My father finally taught me that if you take your time and do it right, you won't have to do it again. If you do it fast, you'll have to do it all over again, and that path will end up taking you longer.

Taking a longer route back to normalcy after an unexpected storm in life is not the most attractive option. It requires patience and sometimes even a more tedious journey. Oftentimes, this is the route that God takes us on. Why does He do that? Because He wants us to achieve His purposes safely, not swiftly.

When you and I experience a setback, our nature is to fight it. We often ask the question, as no doubt the three astronauts did, "I wonder why God has allowed this to happen?"

Have you ever found yourself delayed? Maybe a cancelation or a traffic jam forced you to an alternate plan. Next time that happens, consider, "Maybe God just slowed me down to protect me from something."

Each adversity or setback is a miracle wrapped in disappointment. The shutdowns we experience are often designed to help us rather than destroy us.

God's plan in your life, and God's plan in the church, are inseparable from His all-knowing, strategic timing. Now and then that timing is wrapped in delays, adversity, and challenges. Next time something slows you down or disappoints you, thank God for His hand of protection. Everything happens for a reason.

Also consider this: To know the timing of God is to know His divine plan for your life.

3. God will give you power, even in the absence of perspective. You can receive a demonstration before you will get an explanation. God essentially says, "I control the clock. You just enjoy the journey."

Our impatience with God is like our kids saying, "Are we there yet? Are we there yet?" when we're on a road trip.

To that my wife answers, "When the car stops moving, we will be there. If the car is still moving, we're not there yet, so there is no reason for you to keep asking."

When we say to God, "Are we there yet? Are we there yet?" the Lord answers, though without words, "Hey, the car is still moving. The sun is still rising. The lame are still healed; the lost are still saved. Enjoy the journey!"

We have power. Working power. We can do our best at the task He sets us to do and keep doing our best until He says, "You're there." In the meanwhile, we just trust Him and let God unfold His reasons in His time—if we're meant to know them.

I can get through the bumps and potholes to revival if I just let go of the stopwatch. If I can ride out the storm and trust the timing of God, I can recover from any unexpected event.

God let Pharaoh hang around. He let Lucifer hang around. He has a reason, a purpose, and a time for all things. He may be letting your nemeses hang around, much to your displeasure, but God is the master of timing, and He will get you through it.

Just keep teaching. Just keep reaching. Keep singing. Keep praising. It's going to be worth it all!

4. If God directs the steps, He will direct the finish. The Bible tells us that God is the author *and the finisher* of our faith (Hebrews 12:2). God loves to finish what He starts. He doesn't leave loose ends. We may feel the tyranny of time and wonder what is taking so long, but in the end, God will finish the work.

Aboard Apollo 13, the oxygen tank's faulty sensor had prompted more frequent cryo-stirs. As a result, the explosion that had just happened during the fifth stir occurred at a time when all three astronauts could survive. Yet the crew likely believed the explosion would slow their mission, if not stop it entirely. However, God was directing the steps, and He would also direct the finish. All in God's time.

God's Well-Timed Warning System

In the command module, the explosion set off alarms, both audible and visible. The alarms had been designed to instantly alert the crew to problems so they could immediately begin to address the issues.

God's provision of timing for our lives includes warnings and alarms, which must be heeded, set to alert us at exactly the right moment. To illustrate this point, here is what happened next on April 13, 1970. . . .

Johnson Space Center, Mission Evaluation Room (MER)—April 13, 1970, 9:08 p.m.—the time of the explosion

At his console, engineer Jerry Woodfill went about his day monitoring the caution and warning system of Apollo 13, a system he helped to create. The master alarm flickered for a few moments then glowed bright. He sat upright.

Chaos erupted throughout the room. Woodfill immediately labored to make sense of the readings.

And to think—just a decade before he'd been struggling at Rice University, the recipient of a basketball scholarship. A recipient who, even at this moment, still held the record for the lowest shooting percentage in the history of the university. For Woodfill, basketball and his less-than-stellar grade scores ceased to matter the day President John F. Kennedy had arrived at Rice and delivered a speech. . . .

"But why, some say, the moon? Why choose this as our goal? And they may well ask why climb the highest mountain? Why, thirty-five years ago, fly the Atlantic? Why does Rice play Texas?

"We choose to go to the moon. We choose to go to the moon in this decade and do the other things, not because they are easy, but because they are hard, because that goal will serve to organize and measure the best of our energies and skills, because that challenge is one that we are willing to accept, one we are unwilling to postpone, and one which we intend to win. . . ."

The moon. In the audience, Woodfill was hooked. After the speech he cut his losses on his basketball career and poured himself into his studies of electrical engineering. He wanted the space program to be his future. He wanted to help send astronauts to the moon, and *safely* bring them back to Earth.

> **NASA Trivia:** Which Apollo astronaut was a fighter pilot for ten years and also a test pilot for the first space shuttle, *Enterprise*?[4]
>
> *(See footnote for answer.)*

A Life-Saving Early Warning System

Woodfill developed the Apollo alarm system to function similar to light-up dashboard indicators in an automobile. Check your oil. Your door is ajar. There's a particular malfunction aboard the spacecraft. He prepared an alarm for every conceivable problem that might arise, set to go off the instant that trouble appeared.

Alarm systems are not just confined to spacecraft. They are all around us. They are in our cars, our bodies, and our spirits. We often respond by not responding. We try to tune these alarms out, but with limited success.

My truck has an alarm system that refuses to let me tune it out. I've noticed that sometimes I try to outlast it, thinking it'll stop beeping at some point, but it doesn't. I hear it, but I don't want to listen to it. Yet it is relentless. Finally I give in, not because I want to wear the seatbelt but because I don't want to hear the alarm.

Our bodies respond the same way. If they give us alarms and we ignore the first warning signs, eventually they will make their voices heard. We end up sick from lack of sleep or an unhealthy lifestyle. Yes, we had the warning signs, but we tried to ignore them.

---

[4] Astronaut Fred Haise. His military career started in 1952 at the Naval Air Station in Pensacola, Florida.

The Holy Spirit is an alarm system. He is gentler, but relentless. The conviction to stop that you feel at the moment you engage in the wrong conduct is an alarm system. The shame you feel as you sin is an alarm system. Society tells us to override these alarms, but the warning lights must be heeded.

Often when I fly on commercial airlines, I sit in an exit row. Each time I do, the flight attendant asks us passengers in the exit row if we'll help in the case of an emergency. We all say yes. She then suggests that we read the safety card. Rarely, if ever, does anyone read the card. Ninety percent of the time, I read the card because each plane is configured differently. My fellow passengers in the exit row usually stare at me as I read.

I know why no one reads the card. No one thinks there is going to be an emergency, so no one wants to waste their time. This is the same principle that keeps people living in sin. We don't really believe there's going to be an emergency, so why waste time? We try to convince ourselves, "Jesus isn't coming. The world isn't going to end. There isn't a God or won't be a judgment. There's plenty of time." It would do us well to heed the alarms in our lives, and to learn what we can do to help others respond to the alarms in their lives.

Jerry Woodfill developed the alarm systems on Apollo 13, and once the alarms engaged they helped him to work toward an explanation. Alarms carry clues to the solution. Just like the body's central nervous system is "command central" as the alarm system of the anatomy, we can learn about the root cause of health issues by learning what triggered the alarm.

The most dangerous position of any body or machine is the lack of warning. More precisely, the lack of response to the warning.

In the late 1980s while training for my private pilot's license, I initially had a difficult time holding my altitude. The instructor would tell me, "Let's fly at 2000 feet." I would try to hold that altitude, but I would climb to 2200. Then I'd try to correct it and drop to 1800. Up and down I went. Wasting fuel and time.

The instructor said my problem was that I was looking at the wrong gauge. I was watching the altimeter that tells what altitude you're already at. He said if I would watch the vertical speed indicator, I could see where I was trending and make small corrections *before* I arrived at the wrong altitude. After I learned to watch the early indicators, I could fly straight and avoid a nosedive.

In life, it is often the response to the symptom rather than the cause that makes us constantly have to correct our course after the fact. If we could respond to the early indicators, we could make minor corrections and stay on course.

Our conscience is our life-saving, faith-preserving early-warning system, but it can be overridden. The Holy Spirit is the constant Advisor within each Spirit-filled believer, quickly alerting us of hazardous situations and guiding us to solutions and safer paths on our journeys.

Even in alerting us to sin and danger, God is instantly with us, and His timing is perfect.

God's strategic choice of the best time to alter men's plans and to implement His own, and a wisely conceived alarm system that warned of danger at exactly the right time, saved the lives of astronauts Lovell, Swigert, and Haise.

Apollo 13, miracle number three.

FAITH ACCELERATOR

List events in your life when God's timing did turn out to be exactly right. If ever you find yourself growing impatient with God's plans or pace, review your notes, and praise Him for His all-knowing, strategic timing.

Next, list events in your life when the Holy Spirit alerted you to imminent sin or danger. Once you have, read over them again. Become familiar with and appreciative of God's alarm system that He designed, in love, to help keep you safe. When you experience similar alarms in the future, you will be better equipped to heed them, in God's perfect time.

_____
_____
_____
_____
_____
_____
_____
_____
_____
_____
_____
_____
_____
_____
_____
_____
_____
_____
_____
_____
_____
_____
_____
_____
_____

Mission Control directors discussing options during the Apollo 13 crisis. Credit: NASA.

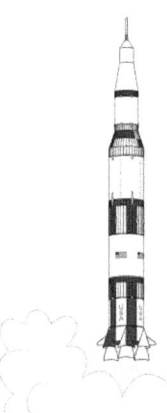

Chapter 4
Hidden Opportunity

Apollo 13 Miracle #4: A Malfunctioning Hatch
April 13, 1970, 9:08 p.m.

An explosion had just blown a thirteen-foot high panel off the exterior of the service module. Neither Lovell, Swigert, Haise nor anyone at Mission Control had any idea yet what had actually happened.

As revealed in his book *Lost Moon*, coauthored with Jeffrey Kluger, Jim Lovell thought the "bang-whump-shudder" that jolted the spacecraft may have been a meteor that struck the lunar module. He realized the LM exterior may have been breached.

Similar to submarine hatches that a crew closes between compartments as soon as the sub has been struck by a depth charge or torpedo, the hatch between the spacecraft's command module and lunar module could be shut if a module was struck by a meteor, so that the oxygen wouldn't empty into space.

Rapidly Lovell told Swigert to close—"button up"—the hatch between the CM and the LM.

Swigert moved to do so. The hatch closed, but it would not stay shut. It refused to latch.

Swigert tried three times, then Lovell tried twice. The hatch would not cooperate. Lovell observed that if the spacecraft were going to depressurize, it would have already.

The men set aside the hatch and shifted their attention back to the gauges and their oxygen supply.

NASA engineer Jerry Woodfill is certain the malfunctioning hatch helped to save the astronauts. The power that the crew would soon discover they needed in order to stay alive waited beyond the door of the hatch they were trying to shut and seal off—in the lunar lander.

If they had sealed the hatch and later tried to reopen it, the amount of power, energy, and oxygen used to complete the task would have further depleted their already crippled life essentials, even if only by a small amount. And they would soon find out that they would have no power to spare.

The fact that the door would not stay shut saved their lives.

Problems: Closed Doors or Future Opportunities?

Have you ever stepped back and looked at something in your life that would not bulge and thought, "Hey, I'm still breathing. I'm still serving God. This thing has not destroyed me. I might as well move on to something else." If that thing won't budge, it may be that God is going to use that situation to help you down the line.

Some doors in our lives that will not close may be miracles in the making.

God controls which doors in life open and shut. When He shuts a door, it is shut. Noah didn't shut the door to the ark; God did. When the door to the ark was shut, it was shut. Only God can open a door after He has chosen to close it.

"To the angel of the church in Philadelphia write:
'These are the words of Him who is holy and true, who holds the key of David. What He opens no one can shut, and what He shuts no one can open'" (Revelation 3:7).

Sometimes God chooses to permanently seal doors in our lives that lead to paths or that continue paths He has strategically chosen to alter.

Sometimes help can come in the form of a door that will not remain shut. God knows that we will need to access that door in the future, like the astronauts discovered.

Other times, doors are shut temporarily. They are future miracles or blessings awaiting your prayer.

Closed Doors That Are Miracles Awaiting Audacious Prayer

We have seen that the Lord is a God of improper miracles—happenings that are physically or scientifically impossible to us. In Acts 4, Peter and John were shut in jail for preaching about the death and resurrection of Jesus. The next morning they would appear before the same key leaders whose actions had led to the torture and crucifixion of Jesus.

"Annas the high priest was there, and so were Caiaphas, John, Alexander and the other men of the high priest's family" (Acts 4:6).

To Peter and John, it may have seemed that God was about to close a rather significant door in their lives.

The next day the Sanhedrin, a council of Jewish leaders, worked together to figure out what to do to the two disciples, because they had healed a previously lame man at the temple. They summarized their dilemma:

"'What are we going to do with these men?' they asked. 'Everybody living in Jerusalem knows they have done an outstanding miracle, and we cannot deny it'" (Acts 4:16).

Sometimes the doors God closes are permanent. Sometimes they are wondrous blessings awaiting prayer.

Miracles: You can't deny when God steps in and performs the impossible. You can't stop it. You can't box it. You can't minimize it with traditions and laws. God challenges our thinking with the unexplainable and the unexpected. Everything is on the table with God, even the things we have taken off the table with our fears and misconceptions.

God wants to decrease our preconceptions and increase our expectations. Those miracles you secretly longed for but were embarrassed to ask God for, I challenge you to stir the embers of that fire. Ask for big things. It's time to think big. Believe big. Anything is possible.

"Now to Him who is able to do immeasurably more than all we ask or imagine, according to His power that is at work within us, to Him be glory . . ." (Ephesians 3:20-21a).

I believe God likes to perform miracles that are out of order. Miracles that are out of season. Events that are outside of the statistical data. Something unprecedented. Something unpredictable. Something that gives hell a headache!

All God needs is some folks crazy enough to ask for, and believe He will grant, the sky. God needs people with difficulties that can't be dismissed with a handshake and a smile.

He needs someone who needs a miracle that is off the charts. Someone who needs an out-of-this-world, out-of-orbit, undeniable, unexplainable miracle.

To believe God will grant something—that takes audacity. You have to get an attitude. "No devil is going to come into my house and take my health, my children, or my stuff without a fight. I won't go quietly. I'm ready to petition for the impossible."

The challenge for each of us in our humanity is this: How do we pray and believe God will allow the blessing to fall from heaven, when we feel the fire of loss or turmoil around us? How do we ride the fire without burning up?

Elijah called fire down from heaven on Mount Carmel and then hid in a cave and wished for death. Times of audacious prayer are when we have to walk after the Spirit and not after the flesh, as Paul describes in Romans. In other words, we must trust our spiritual knowledge rather than the impulses of our flesh. As one preacher said, "Pray the hardest when it is the hardest to pray." The fire of adversity will not hurt a believer who continues to pray, trust, and believe.

Sometimes God permanently closes doors. Sometimes closed doors are miracles awaiting prayer.

The same God who can do the unexplainable can also be silent when all we want is an explanation. The God who works beyond our imagination does not always stoop to our reasoning. Miracles and misery are not always mutually exclusive.

But He hears, cares, and answers prayers. He helps us through.

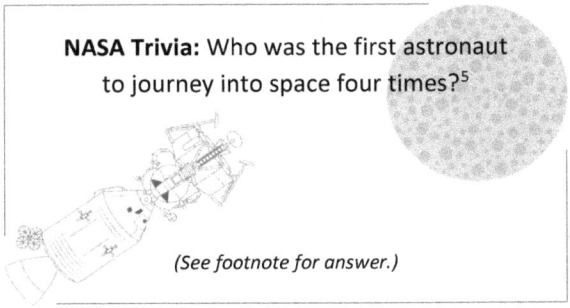

NASA Trivia: Who was the first astronaut to journey into space four times?[5]

(See footnote for answer.)

---

[5] Jim Lovell journeyed into space four times aboard Gemini and Apollo missions. He held the record of traveling 715 hours in space (nearly a month total) until that record was surpassed by the first crew of the Skylab space station in 1973.

Heartache: An Open Door That We Can't Close Alone

Sometimes when faced with a loss or crisis, we try to shut it off, get closure, and move on, but somehow the situation seems to ease back into our lives. We try to shut a door, but God will not allow it to shut.

The desire for closure is often a reaction of the flesh, not of the Spirit. We try to get closure emotionally, mentally, and socially so we can move on. This process is often hindered by God because that gate needs to stay open for some reason we cannot see. The flesh wants to move on, but the Spirit is trying to help us get clarity rather than closure.

Abraham tried to send Hagar and Ismael out of the camp to get closure on his sin. That didn't work out well for Abraham. Thousands of years later, the Jews and Arabs are still fighting, and God will not allow the Jews to shut the door on the Arabs.

Remember two things:
1. God is more merciful than we are.
2. God knows the heart.

Heartache or loss is a door that may not close immediately. But we get tired of heartache. We get tired of rejection. And conflict. And inconsistency. So the flesh says, "Enough is enough!" But God says, "It's not time yet." God may be letting residual pain or people hang around in your life that are driving you crazy. It isn't meant to torture you, but rather to teach trust.

We are to focus on God and His renewal. Deliverance comes by prayer and fasting. Prayer and fasting are part of the dying process.

"'I tell you the truth, unless a kernel of wheat falls to the ground and dies, it remains only a single seed. But if it dies, it produces many seeds'" (John 12:24).

Oftentimes heartache is an open door that we cannot close. God allowed it to be this way, so that we remember to seek out

Him and His healing love. He is the one who can close the door to heartache, in His wise, strategic time.

*"He heals the brokenhearted
and binds up their wounds" (Psalm 147:3).*

"[Jesus] said to her, 'Daughter, your faith has healed you. Go in peace and be freed from your suffering'" (Mark 5:34).

Relinquish the reins of regret to God's healing, and you will be rewarded with renewal and recovery.

Hope: An Open Door That Will Not Close

Like the hatch on Apollo 13, some doors will not stay closed. Here's a way to look at the miracle of gates that stay open.

Hell has been trying to slam the gate on hope from day one, but it keeps opening back up again. Just when a person thinks all hope is lost, God gives us a second chance. And then another. And then another. God is all-loving and immeasurably patient. The gate of hope opens again even when we think we've run out of chances.

Just because a gate appears closed does not mean that God has allowed it to latch.

Hell thought the gate was closed on Calvary—even Jesus said, "It is finished"—but the door soon opened up again when He rose from death. This is why Jesus said, *"'And I tell you that you are Peter, and on this rock I will build My church, and the gates of Hades will not overcome it'" (Matthew 16:18).*

Hope is an open door that will not close. The Lord does not allow the enemy to control the gate.

"He replied, 'Because you have so little faith. I tell you the truth, if you have faith as small as a mustard seed, you can say to this mountain, "Move from here to there" and it will move. Nothing will be impossible for you. But this kind does not go out except by prayer and fasting'" (Matthew 17:20-21).

Unprecedented revival in these last days means a constant renewal. As soon as the enemy gets a victory, there is something about the church that springs back again. There is a constant resurrection. The enemy thinks he has the church down, and he slams the door thinking it is finished . . . and somehow the gate opens back up.

Have you ever had a door like that in your house, or a gate like that in your yard? You slam it shut but it just eases open again. It will drive you crazy. It drives Satan crazy. We can always have hope in God, because God always loves us. Always and forever.

He keeps the gate of hope open for us; we must keep the gate open on our own spirit. Lift up your head, and hold on to hope. God will bless.

> *"Lift up your heads, O you gates;*
> *be lifted up, you ancient doors,*
> *that the King of Glory may come in" (Psalm 24:7, 9).*

An explosion had rocked Apollo 13. Right then, believers in God among the crew and those at Mission Control were likely praying for a miracle.

Though they didn't know it, God had quietly performed one—a hatch that would not close, one that wouldn't block them from reaching the resources they were about to need desperately.

Days later, they would need the hatch to seal. It would.

Apollo 13, miracle number four.

Faith Accelerator

List times when God permanently closed a door to a path you had been on, which forced you to take a new path or to depend on Him. After each entry, note the way or ways in which that closed door proved to be a blessing.

Next, list times when God temporarily closed a door to a path you had been on, which brought about your prayer. After each entry, write the way or ways in which that temporarily closed door proved to be a blessing.

Finally, list events of heartache in your life which God has healed. Thank Him for each one, then pray audaciously for any recent feelings of sadness, suffering, or despair to be healed, and for hope to shine.

_____
_____
_____
_____
_____
_____
_____
_____
_____
_____
_____
_____
_____
_____
_____
_____
_____
_____
_____
_____
_____
_____
_____
_____
_____
_____

The original prime crew for Apollo 13 was Jim Lovell, Ken Mattingly and Fred Haise. Credit: NASA

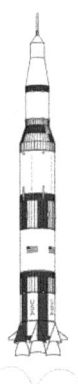

Chapter 5
"There Shall Be Wings!"

"There shall be wings! If the accomplishment be not for me, 'tis for some other. It shall be done!"
—*Leonardo da Vinci, while he stood atop the Mount Albano precipice and watched his carefully designed flying machine crash into the valley below, according to a companion and da Vinci biographer*

Apollo 13 Miracle #5: Measles
April 13, 1970, 9:10 p.m.

Lovell, Swigert, and Haise worked rapidly with Mission Control to understand the reason for the explosion and to try to salvage what remained of their oxygen supply. Jack Swigert wasn't supposed to have been on this mission at all, and now his life was in grave danger, as were the lives of his fellow crewmen.

What were Swigert's thoughts? Did he wish he had stayed in Houston?

Houston, Texas, April 8, 1970—72 hours prior to launch
Charlie Duke, the backup lunar module pilot, contracted measles from one of his children. The primary crew and backup crew were exposed, most notably Ken Mattingly. Mattingly, command module pilot on the primary crew, had never had measles and therefore was not immune.

As a result Mattingly was grounded, and probably felt like an eagle whose wings had just been clipped. An ecstatic Jack Swigert was notified he would replace him.

As a result, Mattingly—a masterful engineer and problem-solver—and Swigert—clear-headed and obsessively precise under extreme stress—were each in exactly the best position for their talents should anything go wrong with the mission.

And now the Apollo 13 mission and crew were in danger. To Jerry Woodfill, it seemed providential—miraculous—that Mattingly had remained in Houston and Swigert was aboard the spacecraft.

Swigert, a former varsity football player for the University of Colorado, had the brawn to withstand the harsh conditions—such as freezing cold and water rationing—that the three astronauts would encounter over the days ahead. Plus, of the nearly thirty astronauts on the Apollo program, Swigert had more knowledge of command and service module malfunction procedures than anyone.

According to Woodfill, "Some have said that Jack had practically written the malfunction procedures for the command module. So, he was the most conversant astronaut for any malfunction that occurred in the CSM" (command and service module). And the role that Mattingly "played in getting the astronauts back home safely can't be overestimated," Woodfill asserted, calling him "an engineer's engineer" due to Mattingly's detailed knowledge of engineering systems and principles, with which Mattingly would help brainstorm solutions to the mission crises at Mission Control. "Remarkably, each man's talents specifically served the unique need."

The best place Swigert could possibly be during this disaster, was on board the spacecraft. And the best place Mattingly could be was at Mission Control. Mattingly's not being immune to a random bout of measles made that happen.

God Uses Setbacks as Setups for the Miraculous

I remember, like it happened yesterday, flipping through the air in my Ford Probe on Interstate 75, on a pitch-black rainy night after having been struck by a drunk driver.

My mind plays it in slow motion: No seatbelt. *Hang on to the steering wheel.* The car rolls over and over. *Try to get control; don't let it land upside down on the interstate. Get out as quickly as possible in case of a fire.*

Finally the car stopped rolling. I crawled out and away, then sat on the side of the road where I listened to emergency vehicles and their sirens coming closer and closer.

There I heard the Lord say, "I spared your life so you would save others through the preaching of the gospel."

God had used the accident to get my attention. Sometime after, I began to see that God often uses apparent setbacks as setups for the miraculous in our lives.

Later, while attending law school and participating in moot court competitions, I had a spirited courtroom exchange with a three-judge panel. I loved it! My adrenaline still pulsed in excitement when I went to the back of the building for a private break. With no one to witness it, I pumped my fist in the air and proclaimed to empty space, "I was made for this!" Immediately the Lord's voice said, "No, you were created to preach the gospel." I repented and remembered what God had said to me after the car accident. Like Ken Mattingly had trained to be on the crew of

Apollo 13, I had trained to become a trial attorney. God had something better in mind for us both.

While composing a letter to the church in Corinth, the apostle Paul plainly listed setbacks he had endured in his ministry.

"Are they servants of Christ? (I am out of my mind to talk like this.) I am more. I have worked much harder, been in prison more frequently, been flogged more severely, and been exposed to death again and again. Five times I received from the Jews the forty lashes minus one. Three times I was beaten with rods, once I was stoned, three times I was shipwrecked, I spent a night and a day in the open sea, I have been constantly on the move. I have been in danger from rivers, in danger from bandits, in danger from my own countrymen, in danger from Gentiles; in danger in the city, in danger in the country, in danger at sea; and in danger from false brothers. I have labored and toiled and have often gone without sleep; I have known hunger and thirst and have often gone without food; I have been cold and naked. Besides everything else, I face daily the pressure of my concern for all the churches" (2 Corinthians 11:23-28).

Such setbacks are not published in promotional materials. They are not included in advertisements for seminary training. But they are very real to anyone who is trying to do more for Christ than just "be saved." Any attempt to expand beyond your own personal salvation and reach others is going to be met with unexpected setbacks.

Paul goes on to state, unequivocally, that the struggles and setbacks were worth it.

"To keep me from becoming conceited because of these surpassingly great revelations, there was given me a thorn in my flesh, a messenger of Satan, to torment me. Three times I pleaded with the Lord to take it away from me. But He said to me, 'My

grace is sufficient for you, for My power is made perfect in weakness.' Therefore I will boast all the more gladly about my weaknesses, so that Christ's power may rest on me. That is why, for Christ's sake, I delight in weaknesses, in insults, in hardships, in persecutions, in difficulties. For when I am weak, then I am strong" (2 Corinthians 12:7-10).

It might not seem like it at the moment, but your perspective of setbacks will help you through immediate disappointments, if you can harness your emotions.

"The heart is deceitful above all things . . ." (Jeremiah 17:9a).

At first glance, it seems strange that Paul *"delight(s) in weaknesses, in insults, in hardships, in persecutions, in difficulties."* Is Paul a few engines short of launch? Does he enjoy suffering? Of course not. Paul means he has found a pattern in serving God and living life: The reward is proportional to the struggle.

In modern speak: no pain, no gain. The wings that God gives us, as da Vinci and the astronauts discovered, are often born in adversity.

Paul points out that these struggles must be *"for Christ's sake."* If we struggle because our own choices and decisions are outside of God's plan or His will, then we're not assured that our efforts will parlay into reward. But if we attempt to follow God's plan for our lives and we're still getting buffeted, we're promised that we will become stronger and more effective.

> *"'As the rain and the snow*
> *come down from heaven,*
> *and do not return to it*
> *without watering the earth*
> *and making it bud and flourish,*

> *so that it yields seed for the sower and bread for the eater,*
> *so is My word that goes out from My mouth:*
> *It will not return to Me empty,*
> *but will accomplish what I desire*
> *and achieve the purpose for which I sent it'"* (Isaiah 55:10-11).

Paul concluded with what appears to be an oxymoron. *"For when I am weak, then I am strong."* This statement wraps up the entire revelation in a nutshell. The weakness of the flesh does not equate to weakness in the spirit. Rather, the opposite is the case. Your renewal is in your rebuttal.

You have to refute even your own emotions.

Turn your setback into a stepping-stone.

Turn your disappointment into deliverance.

Turn your dilemma into a declaration.

Turn your sorrow into a stance.

Determine, *I shall not be moved.*

This is what Job realized.

"And after my skin has been destroyed, yet in my flesh I will see God...." (Job 19:26).

Ask God to develop in you the "setbacks are just setups" mindset. It will enable you to respond to apparent setbacks with, "I will not be moved from my mission."

Here's one more point of "setbacks are just setups" thinking. Paul said, *"There was given me a thorn in my flesh.... Three times I pleaded with the Lord to take it away from me."* The Lord did not remove it at any time in Paul's life. Why? Because God is more concerned about our character than our comfort. He is more concerned about our being saved, than our being satisfied. He wants us to succeed in helping to grow His kingdom, and not turn our focus to pride in ourselves.

We need to overcome frequent setbacks and challenges when touching hearts and lives for eternity. We must focus on God's plan rather than our comforts to make a difference.

True joy comes from serving and equipping others around us.

When we see apparent setbacks as setups, we can press on boldly with the task God has set before us—even if it's not the task *we* think we're best suited for—and draw people closer to God.

"Not only so, but we also rejoice in our sufferings, because we know that suffering produces perseverance; perseverance, character; and character, hope. And hope does not disappoint us, because God has poured out His love into our hearts by the Holy Spirit, whom He has given us" (Romans 5:3-5).

God Uses Setbacks as Setups for Spiritual Renewal

The New Testament church that we read about in the book of Acts is familiar with setbacks. Unexpected events were the norm. They had to learn to expect the unexpected. They also learned that renewal of faith starts out, first and foremost, with adversity. For Peter, setbacks sometimes meant prison.

"Suddenly an angel of the Lord appeared and a light shone in the cell. He struck Peter on the side and woke him up. 'Quick, get up!' he said, and the chains fell off Peter's wrists.

Then the angel said to him, 'Put on your clothes and sandals.' And Peter did so. 'Wrap your cloak around you and follow me,' the angel told him. Peter followed him out of the prison, but he had no idea that what the angel was doing was really happening; he thought he was seeing a vision. They passed the first and second guards and came to the iron gate leading to the city. It opened for them by itself, and they went through it. When they had walked the length of one street, suddenly the angel left him.

Then Peter came to himself and said, 'Now I know without a doubt that the Lord sent His angel and rescued me from Herod's clutches and from everything the Jewish people were anticipating'" (Acts 12:7-11).

The pattern of adversity and renewal is clear from the very beginning and carries through all the way to Calvary. Something dies, that death brings a burial, and then a resurrection. It happened in creation with the seasons, and in the great flood. It defined the people of Israel, and was modeled by the life of Jesus. It played out in the New Testament church, and the ministry of Paul. And it is the plan of salvation.

Adversity is followed by renewal. Death, burial, and then resurrection.

The New Testament church knew they were a people of destiny, but each step they took, adversity became stronger. In Acts 4, Peter and John are imprisoned. In Acts 5, two charter members of the church are killed by God. In Acts 7, a promising young preacher named Stephen is stoned to death while preaching. In Acts 10, Peter goes to the house of a Roman centurion.
In Acts 12, John the Baptist is beheaded, and Peter goes back to prison.

This does not appear to be an illustrious beginning for a new church plant.

No doubt, these events were not anticipated when the followers of Jesus rejoiced over 3000 people being added to the church in one day. What if the New Testament believers had stopped there and said, "No more!"? What if they had allowed those challenges to eliminate their future?

The book of Acts could have been limited to a collage of hard challenges, but the early church persevered. In fact, Acts 5 records believers' reaction to adversity.

"The apostles left the Sanhedrin, rejoicing because they had been counted worthy of suffering disgrace for the Name. Day after day, in the temple courts and from house to house, they never stopped teaching and proclaiming the good news that Jesus is the Christ" (Acts 5:41-42).

Why did they do this? There can only be one answer: They recognized each setback as a precursor to renewal. One of the keys to personal renewal is to understand that setback is a setup for *spiritual* growth.

God permitted Peter to be imprisoned and to face the threat of a trial and sentencing in front of Herod come morning. Instead of unending trouble, God renewed Peter. Peter would face future trials, but he would also be blessed with future renewals of body, mind, and spirit. He would experience men's sudden attacks, and then God's miraculous deliverances.

If you live in the environment of persecution, you learn that prayer is not optional. Unprecedented renewal comes about by constant prayer.

"So Peter was kept in prison, but the church was earnestly praying to God for him" (Acts 12:5).

It is hurt that hones this kind of recovery and conviction. This is where renewal comes from. It is forged in the fire of adversity.

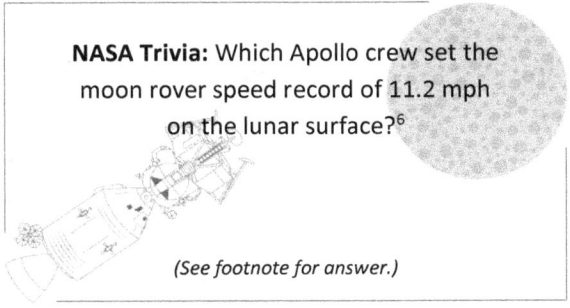

NASA Trivia: Which Apollo crew set the moon rover speed record of 11.2 mph on the lunar surface?[6]

(See footnote for answer.)

---

[6] The crew of Apollo 16. Currently the fastest person on Earth can sprint 23.35 mph—more than twice the speed of the moon rover.

God Gives Each of Us His or Her Own Wings

"To You, O Lord, I lift up my soul . . ." (Psalm 25:1).

The word *lift* is associated with many things in our culture. In England, they don't call their underground trains "subways." They call them the "Tube." They call an elevator a "lift."

The word is used more often as a verb than a noun. As a verb *lift* means "to direct or carry from a lower to a higher position. To raise. To elevate. To rise or cause to rise upward from the ground or another support to a higher place."

As a noun it means "the act or process of raising to a higher position."

In aeronautics we student pilots learned that lift is the force that directly opposes the weight of an airplane. Lift is the component of aerodynamic force that is perpendicular to the relative wind. *Drag* is the component of aerodynamic force that is parallel to the relative wind. Lift counteracts weight, and thrust counteracts drag, and that is how a plane flies.

Suffice it to say, lift holds the airplane in the sky. If the plane ceases to lift, it ceases to fly.

Hebrews 12:1 tells us we should lay aside every weight and sin that hinders us. We know what sin is, but what about this weight? Weight is the cares of life. The woes. The blues. However you want to describe it. Life has a lot of weight. A lot of heaviness.

I believe that natural laws illustrate spiritual laws. I wrote a book about how man's laws illustrate spiritual laws, but an even greater analogy is how natural laws illustrate spiritual laws, because they have the same Author.

If we are to counteract the weight in life, the heaviness in life, the pain and sorrow, we must lift. Lift up your head. Lift up your eyes. Lift up your soul. Lift up your hands. Lift up your voice. Lift up your Lord.

Lift. Elevate. Raise the roof in prayer and praise, even amid apparent setbacks.

When we do that, God gives us wings. Wings with which to overcome our setbacks, and to triumph within what God has set up.

To continue the airplane analogy, when the wind hits the front of an airplane, it hits the leading edge of the wing. When it does this, the wind splits. Some of the wind goes over the top of the wing, and some goes under. They meet once again on the trailing edge of the wing.

The wing is designed so that the wind that goes over the top has a greater distance to travel because of the camber (or design of the wing) than the wind cutting under. The wind cutting under has a shorter distance to travel, so it speeds up. The wind on top can't keep up because it has a longer distance to travel.

The faster wind on the bottom of the wing creates greater pressure than the wind on the top. As the pressure becomes greater on the bottom than the top, it starts to counteract the weight. This is what happens as you speed down the runway. When you reach rotation (the speed at which the plane begins to lift), the pressure is sufficient under the wing to lift, then you pull back on the yoke and away you go.

The greater the weight, the more pressure is needed to get lift, and the longer the runway needs to be to build up that pressure.

The more I worship God, the greater pressure it puts on hell.

Hell wants to put all the pressure on you so you never get off the ground. You walk around with your head down, your heart broken. Beaten. Broken. Grounded. That is what weight and sin do.

But if I lift up the Lord, the pressure begins to change. If I give God quick access to my heart and make the devil take the long road, the pressure changes.

If I lift up the Lord, then my own head begins to lift. My own heart begins to lift.

Let me make one other point here. You can't get lift without wind. You need adversity to get elevation. The harder the wind is blowing against you, the quicker you can get lift. That is why planes always take off into the wind.

You might think, "I could worship God if I didn't have so many problems." The opposite is true.

Turn your problems into praise makers.

Turn your woes into worship.

Turn your headaches into high praise.

The Bible talks about "high praise" (Psalm 149:6, various versions). People always debate what high praise is. I think high praise is praise in the middle of adversity.

The greater the opposing force, the higher we go. The greater the wind, the higher we go.

Have you ever seen an eagle ride on the currents of a storm? Everything else in nature runs for cover, but an eagle with its seven-foot wing span will soar in a storm.

> "But those who hope in the Lord
> will renew their strength.
> They will soar on wings like eagles;
> they will run and not grow weary,
> they will walk and not be faint" (Isaiah 40:31).

When Job was beside himself with grief and despair, to the point that he questioned God, God asked Job, *"'Does the eagle soar at your command and build his nest on high?'" (Job 39:27)*. That verse reveals two things.

1. The eagle doesn't need anybody to tell him to mount up. "Get your wings out; it's time to fly." The eagle doesn't need anyone or anything to encourage it.

We should be able to lift up the Lord without any help. We should not need music to get us going. We should not need lights and videos and special effects. We should not need a pat on the back.

I lift. That's just who I am. It is my nature to worship God. I worship Him in the good and the bad. I worship Him by where I go, and what I do, and how I talk, and what I wear.

I lift.

2. The eagle makes its nest on high. It's time to take the high ground. Every time Old Testament people put up false idols to worship, they always tried to put them up on high ground. The enemy is always wanting to get on high ground. Over and over we read in the Old Testament, there were high places.

There is a military and spiritual advantage to being on the high ground. When you worship God, you climb to higher ground. David said (emphasis added):

"I will be glad and rejoice in You;
*I will sing praise to Your name, O **Most High** . . ." (Psalm 9:2).*

"There is a river whose streams make glad the city of God,
*the holy place where the **Most High** dwells" (Psalm 46:4).*

*"Your righteousness reaches **to the skies**, O God,*
you who have done great things.
Who, O God, is like You?" (Psalm 71:19).

God told Moses, When you come out of Egypt, come out with a high hand.

God also told Moses, "Lift up your rod and stretch it out over the sea," and then the children of Israel walked over on dry ground.

In the ministry of Jesus, He was lifted up in the wilderness and was yet without sin.

At the Jordan River, John the Baptist lifted up his eyes and said, *"'Look, the Lamb of God, who takes away the sin of the world!'" (John 1:29b).*

At Calvary, Jesus was lifted up on the cross and then crucified.

Trials and troubles followed Jesus during His ministry, but every vision people had of Him after the resurrection was one of Jesus lifted up. Stephen saw Him high in heaven sitting on the right hand of power. Paul saw Him on high. John saw Him high on a throne.

His disciples were led to assemble in a high place. Suddenly there came a sound from heaven like a rushing, mighty wind! Soon after, God gave them spiritual wings.

God often uses apparent setbacks as setups for the miraculous in our lives.

God Gives You Your Wings

It's amazing to me how the Lord orchestrates even the smallest of details in our lives to equip us for the perfect will of God. He hand-selected for each one of us our unique appearance and personality. He also gives us our unique abilities—our own wings.

"'Before I formed you in the womb I knew you . . .'" (Jeremiah 1:5a).

Just as God equipped the NASA team with exactly the skill sets they needed, He has equipped each of us for our individual journeys. Oftentimes we think someone else is better looking, or more intelligent, capable, or successful, or more blessed in some way. This is a trick of the enemy—the longest living expert on human psychology and weaknesses outside of God—who whispers doubt and turns our attention to ourselves instead of to the specialized abilities and mission God has blessed us with. No one can be a better you.

"In Him we were also chosen, having been predestined according to the plan of Him who works out everything in conformity with the purpose of His will . . ." (Ephesians 1:11).

God has given you your own purpose. And He has or will inspire your dreams and goals so that you're drawn to them to achieve them. Like Woodfill, our desire should not be to claim a historical or some other spotlight, but to fly with the wings God has given us, and to help others fly with theirs. We may be in the spotlight. We may be in the shadows. Fulfill your purpose wherever you are, and give God the glory. Only then will your cup of joy run over.

Swigert's physiology, exceptional knowledge of malfunction procedures, and near-obsessive attention to detail made him the best man to work the problem from the command module. Mattingly was scrubbed from the mission, but his life was saved, and his unexpected setback, which placed him and his advanced engineering and problem-solving skills precisely where they were needed most, helped save the lives of Lovell, Swigert, and Haise.

And that because of Charlie Duke's measles—an apparent setback that set up a miracle.

Apollo 13, miracle number five.

FAITH ACCELERATOR

List setbacks that have happened in your life when you reached out to others with the message of God's presence, love, and salvation. After each entry, write ways in which God enabled you to become stronger and more effective as a result. Incidents of strength and greater effectiveness will likely include greater faith.

In the future when you face an apparent setback, reread your notes. Then praise God and lift Him up, because the setback may very well be a setup for a miracle.

_____

_____

_____

_____

*Apollo 13 Flight Director Gene Kranz
working the problem at Mission Control.
Credit: NASA.*

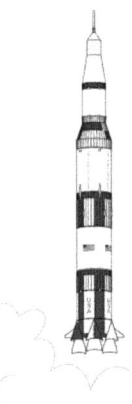

Chapter 6
Attitude and Guts

Powering Up
April 13, 1970, 9:46 p.m.

As soon as the extent of damage caused by the O2 tank explosion had been realized, Lovell, Swigert, and Haise had begun an emergency power down of the command and service module (CSM) and a power up of the lunar module. The LM contained enough fuel, power, and oxygen to serve as a lifeboat until the crew could approach Earth's atmosphere for reentry.

At 11:53 p.m., all CSM systems were powered down and all LM systems powered up. With the astronauts out of immediate danger, Mission Control turned its collective attention to the question of how to get the men home.

The original mission was aborted. The new mission was to rescue lives.

Apollo 13 Miracle #6: A Gut Feeling

Flight Director Gene Kranz gathered with his team at Mission Control to decide the next critical question: What was best way to get the astronauts home? An involved discussion presented two options: the fastest way possible, or the safest way possible.

Apollo 13 had already traversed more than half the distance to the moon. The fastest way home would mean a turn-around between the moon and Earth using the service module's service propulsion system (SPS), the engine that had been designed to provide two key burns: one, to send the spacecraft into lunar orbit, and two, after the lunar orbit had been completed, to direct the spacecraft back toward Earth. However, the SPS may have been damaged, perforated by shrapnel, in the explosion.

The safest way was also the longest—a free-return trajectory around the back of the moon. This would require using the descent engine on the lunar module to direct Apollo 13 into a partial orbit and then the moon's gravity to turn and "slingshot" the spacecraft back toward Earth.

The downside of this option was that this single burn would return the crew to Earth roughly 153 hours after launch—four to five days from this point. With only 154 hours of consumables aboard, this would leave only one extra hour's worth of consumables for the men, an uncomfortably thin margin, even if no additional problems arose.

Once the engineers completed their calculations and determined the engine of the lunar module could perform the necessary burn, the men voiced their choices for the method of return they favored. As Gene Kranz listened to the viewpoints, votes that supported the fast return using the SPS engine struck Kranz with acute foreboding. His gut told him to choose the safer option—to use the engine on the LM to take Apollo 13 the longer way, around the moon.

On April 14, 1970, at 2:42 a.m., the astronauts initiated a midcourse correction using the LM systems for a controlled burn. Soon after, they shut down the engine, now on course for a partial lunar orbit.

In time, Gene Kranz's gut feeling would prove to be right.

"Failure Is Not an Option"

Jerry Bostick—the flight dynamics officer (FDO), or flight controller, of the mission—authored a statement that has never been forgotten. As the engineers tried to figure out a way to get the men home, the extreme challenges of the situation permeated their room at Mission Control.

Bostick reminded the team, "Failure is not an option." More recently Bostick has explained, "When bad things happened, we just calmly laid out all the options, and failure was not one of them. We never panicked, and we never gave up on finding a solution.

"For us engineers in the control room, it was a religious experience," he added. "The rescue of these three men against all odds increased my faith in God. But it did not start with Apollo 13. I first felt the hand of God on Apollo 8, when they first came around from the back side of the moon the first time at the exact second we had predicted. I teared up and told my colleagues, 'This just proves that Someone is in charge who knows a lot more about orbital mechanics than any of us.'"

Many men who worked on the early Apollo program experienced their faith in God grow with each success, but their faith grew even stronger with each failure. They learned firsthand that failure is not a part of God's nature. It is the nature of man when he attempts to be independent of God.

Failure Is Not an Option with God

Deuteronomy 31:6 and Joshua 1:5 show us that it is not in the nature of God to fail. Beyond the nature of God to not fail, is the nature of God that He has imparted to us, the church.

"'Be strong and courageous. Do not be afraid or terrified because of them, for the Lord your God goes with you; He will never leave you nor forsake you'" (Deuteronomy 31:6).

"'No one will be able to stand up against you all the days of your life. As I was with Moses, so I will be with you; I will never leave you nor forsake you'" (Joshua 1:5).

Failure Is Not an Option with the Word of God

God reveals His unfailing nature through the Bible.

"In the beginning was the Word, and the Word was with God, and the Word was God. He was with God in the beginning. Through Him all things were made; without Him nothing was made that has been made. In Him was life . . ." (John 1:1-4a).

"'Heaven and earth will pass away, but My words will never pass away'" (Matthew 24:35).

Failure Is Not an Option with the Church

The church of God—the timeless, borderless fellowship of believers—does not fail, because of ongoing faith in Him. This church has triumphed. It has been through the fire. It has been through the storm. It is built on the Rock.

God is coming back for His church, His bride. God is coming back for a people who are without spot or wrinkle (Ephesians 5:27).

Ephesians 5:27 is the only place in the Bible where the word "wrinkle" is found. Wrinkle indicates a flaw or a lack of perfection. No doubt, we are less than perfect, but our wrinkle-free resurrection is the result of the flawless nature of God's cleansing blood.

Failure Is Not an Option with the Holy Spirit

The absence of failure is not limited to God's nature, His Word, and His church. When God puts His Holy Spirit in you, He gives you a nature that is like His. Part of recovering from a disappointment or catastrophe is to come to the determination that quitting one's faith, or one's God-given mission, is not an option. "I may stumble, but I'm going to get back up on my feet because I will not fail. It is not an option. I'm going to make it. Sin will not win. I will find a way to win. I will find a way to succeed."

To succeed after life's setbacks, you've got to get some gumption. You've got to get some grit. You've got to get some determination. "Devil, you may have knocked me down, but I am going to get back up, because failure is not an option."

Failure Is Not an Option: The Attitude of Successful Action

Consider three steps that turn the above attitude of success into action.

1. Pursuit

"And David inquired of the Lord, 'Shall I pursue this raiding party? Will I overtake them?'

'Pursue them,' He answered. 'You will certainly overtake them and succeed in the rescue'" (1 Samuel 30:8).

For failure to not be an option, success must be pursued. Pursuing is putting feet on your faith. If you believe God will give you the victory, then you will pursue your dreams and goals.

In Mark 10:46, blind Bartimaeus had reached a point where failure was not an option to him. The idea of living blind one more day was not acceptable.

"When he heard that it was Jesus of Nazareth, he began to shout, 'Jesus, Son of David, have mercy on me!'" (Mark 10:47).

People nearby told the man to keep quiet, but pursuit requires action in the face of adversity.

You will not always have a crowd cheering you on. You may have a crowd that is nonresponsive or even jeering you. Pursuit requires action no matter what.

2. Persistence

"Many rebuked him and told him to be quiet, but he shouted all the more, 'Son of David, have mercy on me!'" (Mark 10:48).

Persistence is repeated pursuit. Persistence requires that you firmly believe—and continue to believe—that failure is not an option. Persistence means that you will not quit until you succeed.

Few things can guarantee success like persistence.

"But those who hope in the Lord
will renew their strength.
They will soar on wings like eagles;
they will run and not grow weary,
they will walk and not be faint" (Isaiah 40:31).

Sometimes you don't have the strength to run or mount up on the wings of eagles. You're just trying to survive. To put one foot in front of the other. To get through the day. In those times, you have to just "walk and not faint."

Unexpected "explosions" can smother your desire to push toward your dream. They can cause you to question everything. God's unfailing nature, love, and power is the deep well that you have to draw from that gives you strength to walk and not faint.

3. Passion

Perhaps those who were near Bartimaeus when he cried out for Jesus' healing chided the man by asking, "Why are you making so much noise, Bartimaeus?" I can hear Bartimaeus respond, "Because I'm tired of being blind, and this is my only chance. I'm not going back the way I came! *Jesus, Son of David!*"

You want revival. You want a miracle. Get desperate. Passion is pursuing, with emotion.

Jacob wrestled all night with "an angel of the Lord"—a theophany of God. Jacob told Him, *"'I will not let You go unless*

You bless me'" (Genesis 32:26b). Essentially, "I know this may be unorthodox, but I want my blessing!"

Hannah prayed with such passion in the temple that the high priest thought she was drunk. He told her to get rid of her wine. She basically answered, "I don't care what people think. I want a baby" (1 Samuel 1:13).

Paul witnessed with such intensity before the Roman governor Festus and the Jewish king Agrippa that they thought he was mad (Acts 26:24).

Pursue persistently, with passion.

The men and women of NASA did. As a result, they made it to the moon and beyond.

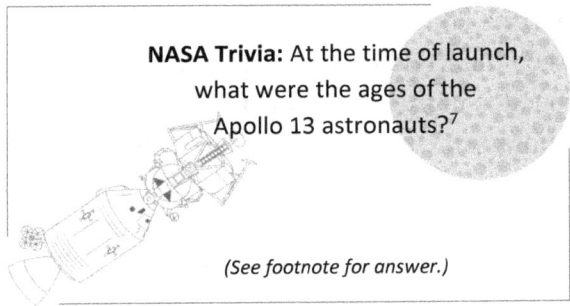

NASA Trivia: At the time of launch, what were the ages of the Apollo 13 astronauts?[7]

(See footnote for answer.)

Stand in the storm of challenge with a declaration that failure is not an option. The storm before you may look nearly impossible to withstand. But with God, all things are possible.

"Jesus looked at them and said, 'With man this is impossible, but with God all things are possible'" (Matthew 19:26).

"He replied, 'Because you have so little faith. I tell you the truth, if you have faith as small as a mustard seed, you can say to this mountain, "Move from here to there" and it will move. Nothing will be impossible for you'" (Matthew 17:20).

---

[7] Jim Lovell was forty-two, Jack Swigert was thirty-eight, and Fred Haise was thirty-six.

The transfer of the nature of God to the children of God through the Holy Spirit includes a fortitude that refuses failure.

The Long Way Home

Yes, even inspired by the Holy Spirit, the journey through life is still difficult. There are days when we have questions and doubts, but still we stand.

With life comes a lot of unexpected events and delays, but taking the long way home is the path that reveals the *keeping power of God.*

How do parents recover from losing a child? I'm not sure if there is anything on Earth and in our humanity that could be tougher than that. I've comforted parents as they processed the loss of a child. I've seen their bodies shake and quiver as the emotional explosion reverberates in their innermost beings.

I have seen those same people square their shoulders and sturdy their stance. An inner peace comes over them. A well of water. I'm not sure how they do it. They find something that others may never have to look for. They dig in deep wells and find a faithful God.

Unchanging faithfulness—that is the keeping power of God.

And since He lives in us, we are not immune to the effects of Calvary.

"I have been crucified with Christ and I no longer live, but Christ lives in me. The life I live in the body, I live by faith in the Son of God, who loved me and gave Himself for me" (Galatians 2:20).

In his book *Not I, But Christ*, Stephen Olford writes, "Christians adore the cradle of Christ and await the coming of Christ, but they abhor the cross of Christ."

The cross is the long way home. It is learning that pain crosses every path but if I embrace it, I can find victory in the night.

"If we have been united with Him like this in His death, we will certainly also be united with Him in His resurrection." (Romans 6:5).

The planting together with Christ in the likeness of His death assures us that we can also share in the likeness of His resurrection.

The cross was not an isolated event. It is the path for each of us. It is learning to use the power of the lunar orbit to slingshot you home rather than risking your own power that has already faltered. The moon shines in the night. The hand of God is most prevalent in the darkness.

It seems that God takes pleasure in making something out of nothing. It only took till the second verse of the Bible to point that out.

"Now the earth was formless and empty . . ." (Genesis 1:2a).

Shortly thereafter, God gathered dust, blew on it, and man was created. He hung the heavens and spread the stars on nothing.

This fact is not lost on Job.

"He spreads out the northern [skies] over empty space;
he suspends the earth over nothing" (Job 26:7).

Have you ever been faced with the decision of two routes that you could take to get home? One you are familiar with. You know it will get you home. The other you are unsure of, but it could possibly be faster. Or it might leave you lost and confused. When faced with these decisions, which route do you choose to take?

"There is a way that seems right to a man,
but in the end it leads to death" (Proverbs 16:25).

When it comes to making heaven your home, go with the route that you know will get you there safely. The route that is tried and true. The route that is based on following the entire Bible, not just part of it.

The path to heaven is not an escalator, or an elevator with buttons labeled Pearly Gates. It is stairs. It is a process of getting tired and still going. It is a process of not understanding everything on this Earth but trusting God anyway.

I will never forget leaving Home Depot one summer day several years ago. My cart was stacked with fence sections, and I loaded the unwieldy fencing into the back of my truck. Two elderly men came out and watched me struggle with the fence sections. I realized my cart was blocking them from being able to back their vehicle out. I apologized and tried to reposition my cart out of their way. One of the elderly men said to me something I've never forgotten. "Son, don't worry about it," he said. "We're not in a hurry. People who are in a hurry are in the ground."

I suppose one reason his statement has always stuck with me is because I feel like I'm always in a hurry. Things just don't move fast enough. It certainly seems that way when you're young. Stairs, not escalators. The older you get, the faster life seems to move. The years give you wisdom that "speed does not equate to safe passage." The statement from these gentlemen also begs the question, "Why are we always in a hurry to go nowhere?"

The key question that each of us must ask in our walk with God is, "Do I take the safest route to heaven or do I take the fastest?" Many times, the fastest route is the most favorable to the flesh, but it's not the safest route. Certainly not for the salvation of the flesh.

I remember my father illustrating this principle with the story of a man who was attempting to land a job as a chauffeur of a rich man. During the driving test, the young man wanted to prove his driving skills by getting as close to the edge of the cliff as possible without sending the car and its passengers over the ravine. The next driver came to the same place and hugged the car as far to the other side of the drop-off as possible. The second driver was older and his reflexes may not have been as good as the younger driver's, but his wisdom and caution won him the job.

I'm pretty sure there are things in my life and things in your life that each of us refrains from, that we could still partake of and probably make it to heaven, but why take a chance?

I'll take the long way home to make sure I get home.

In the teachings of Jesus, our Lord gives us a description of a true disciple by saying, *"'If someone forces you to go one mile, go with him two miles'" (Matthew 5:41)*. I'm sure this wasn't popular when it was spoken, and perhaps it's even less popular now, but it's clearly an example of taking the long way home.

I believe that you can boil down everything that we do in our ministries and Christian spiritual pursuits to one single mission: It is imperative that we make it to heaven safely.

Like the Apollo 13 crew was trying to get back to Earth safely, we are trying to get to heaven safely, even if it requires the longer road.

The enemy of our soul—the great tempter, the one who is a committed adversary to our getting to heaven—will always present an alternate path, and this alternate path will always appear to be a shortcut. It is more attractive. It involves instant gratification. But it is a false road.

Keep your feet on God's path. It is the long, narrow way to success in life and to our home in heaven.

The team at Mission Control never panicked nor stopped working to find solutions. If I can hitch my wagon to the Creator of this universe, I can also proclaim in every situation I face, "Failure is not an option," no matter how long the road.

Around the Moon

After the LM course-correction engine burn sent the spacecraft into a partial lunar orbit, the team at Mission Control realized the critical need for the astronauts to conserve battery power. As a result, the astronauts exited their partial orbit of the moon and had to shut down the LM power systems, including the heat source that until now had kept them warm.

But Lovell, Swigert, and Haise were still alive and were headed toward home, because Gene Kranz had listened to his gut.
Apollo 13, miracle number six.

FAITH ACCELERATOR

List dreams or goals you have *pursued persistently*, with *passion* and achieved. Based on this chapter's descriptions of pursuit, persistence, and passion, briefly describe how each of these three steps brought about your positive results.

Next, note ways in which God has enabled you, or even emboldened you, to succeed.

Finally, pray for His continued infusion of the knowledge that with God as your copilot, "failure is not an option."

_____
_____
_____
_____
_____
_____
_____
_____
_____
_____
_____
_____

Apollo 13 command and service module being moved to integrated workstand for final mating to spacecraft launch adapter. December 10, 1969. Credit: NASA.

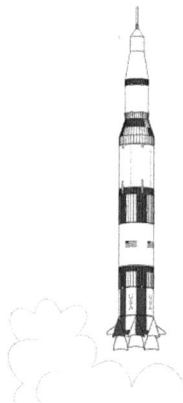

Chapter 7
An Empowered Mission

Apollo 13 Miracle #7: *Marooned*

Astronauts Lovell, Swigert, and Haise shivered in the cold, dark lunar module lifeboat that drifted through the vastness of space in the direction of Earth. All power had been shut off to conserve what battery power remained for eventual reentry into Earth's atmosphere.

Now the men floated weightlessly in the lunar module, their eyes and minds not far from the depleted batteries they would need in order to return home.

Houston, Texas, near the Johnson Space Center, April 13, 1970, a few short hours before Apollo 13's oxygen tank explosion

Jerry Woodfill's fellow NASA engineer Art Campos was intrigued by the fictional story told in the 1964 novel *Marooned* by Martin Caidin. It was a realistic tale of three astronauts who experienced an accident in space aboard an Apollo-like spacecraft. The trio's lives remained in suspenseful jeopardy while NASA engineers labored to find a way to bring the crew back to Earth.

Chapter 7

With the story fresh in his mind, Campos went to bed, his engineer's mind churning a scene about depleted emergency batteries. To correct the depletion problem, the fictional astronauts were instructed to charge the batteries. Campos wondered what his real-life NASA team would do if such a dire situation were to occur during an actual mission.

Shortly after Campos drifted off to sleep, he was awakened by the ringing of his telephone.

"Such a dire situation" had just occurred on board Apollo 13. Campos was instructed to come immediately to the Mission Evaluation Room (MER) and to help find a way to get power to the command module emergency batteries. Without the additional power, Lovell, Swigert, and Haise wouldn't be able to achieve reentry.

At MER, Campos recalled the story, as well as a process he'd formulated months earlier to transfer a battery charge via a set of jumper wires, not unlike jumper cables one would use to charge a car battery. Now, while Campos drafted the procedure, Woodfill and the team created the schematics, their hopes high.

Hope = Mission Possible

If I can keep my hopes alive! If I can keep my faith from faltering! If I can give God access to my heart, then the King will come in! And He helps us keep the batteries of our hearts connected to Him, like a spiritual charge across jumper wires.

> *"'If ye love Me, keep My commandments. And I will pray the Father, and He shall give you another Comforter, that He may abide with you for ever; even the Spirit of truth; whom the world cannot receive, because it seeth Him not, neither knoweth Him: but ye know Him; for He dwelleth with you, and shall be in you'" (John 14:15-17 KJV).*

In the days of the Old Testament, Syria's army was the most vicious in the world. Everyone, except the people of God, feared the Syrian army. During the time Elisha served as God's prophet in Israel, the king of Syria grew frustrated—every battle plan he drew up was being revealed to his enemy before he could fully implement it. When he demanded an explanation from his advisors, they told him, "Israel's God tells their prophet Elisha everything we do."

In response, the king of Syria sent an army to surround Elisha's house.

As dawn lightened the morning sky, Elisha's servant walked out onto the balcony to greet the day. What greeted him was a hostile army of Syrians. Panicked, the servant called for Elisha.

Elisha likewise walked out onto the balcony. He remained remarkably calm.

The servant asked, "Sir, don't you see that army?!"

"Yes, isn't that something," Elisha replied.

"Indeed it is, and what are we going to do about it?"

"And Elisha prayed, 'O Lord, open his eyes so he may see.' Then the Lord opened the servant's eyes, and he looked and saw the hills full of horses and chariots of fire all around Elisha" (2 Kings 6:17).

Not jumper wires, but still a power charge from the King of Glory, and a good reason for Elisha's servant to hope. The mission God gives us to fulfill is *mission possible*—we can have hope that if God brings us to it, He will help us through it.

Elisha said to his servant, "Let's have some fun. Lord, strike the army with blindness." Instantly all the soldiers were blind. Elisha went down to meet them. "Hey, fellas, can I help you?"

"Yeah, we're looking for Elisha," replied the general who was now blind.

"Oh come this way," Elisha said. He led them into the center of the city of Samaria. Blind, the soldiers staggered, holding on to each other. "No, this way, over here, follow my voice!"

I can just hear the servant giggle while Elisha led the soldiers like children. Finally Elisha prayed for the soldiers' eyes to be opened.

At once they could see . . . and realized they were surrounded, in an enemy city. The Syrian army was struck with fear.

The king of Samaria asked Elisha, "Should we kill them?"

Elisha said, "No, feed them and send them home" (2 Kings 6).

Elisha was on an empowered mission. God's mission. And since Elisha walked with God, he had hope.

Hope equals mission *possible*.

At a man's request, God caused the sun to stand still (Joshua 10:12-13). He enabled Elijah to outrun a racing chariot (1 Kings 18:46). At a man's request, God rolled the sun backward in the sky (2 Kings 20:11).

Those who lived with sure hope in God's blessing experienced an empowered mission.

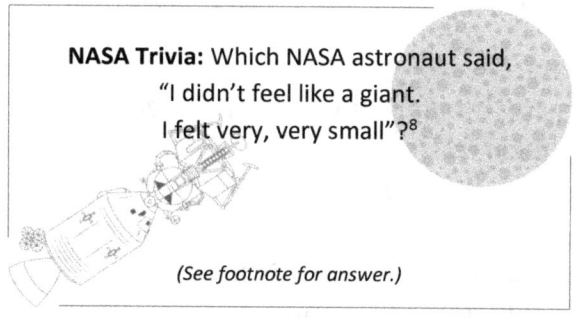

NASA Trivia: Which NASA astronaut said, "I didn't feel like a giant. I felt very, very small"?[8]

(See footnote for answer.)

---

[8] Neil Armstrong, as he recalled standing on the moon and looking back at Earth in July 1969. (During the 1971 Apollo 14 mission, Alan Shepard had a similar reaction. He said, "When I first looked back at the Earth, standing on the moon, I cried.")

God Empowers Your Mission

Life has hurt and pain built in. It's just a part of life, but it's also the greatest time to learn. It's important to tie your spiritual battery onto God and let Him empower your mission.

In the Old Testament book of Ruth, an older woman named Naomi lost her husband and both sons to death. She prepared to return to her homeland, and said good-bye to her two daughters-in-law. One daughter-in-law, Ruth, wouldn't say good-bye to Naomi. She determined to travel and stay with her, like a daughter would her mother, even when Naomi urged Ruth to return to her own people.

"But Ruth replied, 'Don't urge me to leave you or to turn back from you. Where you go I will go, and where you stay I will stay. Your people will be my people and your God my God'" (Ruth 1:16).

Ruth had something in common with NASA engineers—they all had the same God empowering their mission.

Here are three ways Ruth hooked into that Power Source, which we can emulate.

1. Commit yourself to the journey. Before God ever reveals Himself to you in an intimate relationship, He wants to know you will follow Him through thick and thin. Are you only in the relationship for the fishes and the loaves? Are you only in it for what you can get out of it? Ruth determined to worship Naomi's God before she fully knew Him. She committed herself to the journey.

Just before Jesus ascended into heaven, He asked Peter, "Peter, do you love Me?" Jesus asked Peter the same question *three* times. Why three? Jesus had to sink a message into Peter's head: "You have to get this first. You have to get this before you can get revelation, before your mission can be empowered. You are going to have many opportunities to leave Me. You are going to have more opportunities to deny Me. Peter, commit yourself to this."

I believe one of the biggest crises in Christianity today is lack of commitment. We will only walk with God while it's convenient. We will only attend church if it fits our schedules. As soon as the wind blows, as soon as I get my feelings hurt, I am out of there.

The Bible is shouting instructions to us: Commit yourself to the journey. Put your hand on the plow and don't look back. You will have many opportunities. You will have many excuses. You will want to quit on a regular basis.

Commit yourself to the journey, and God will empower your mission.

2. Stop and worship. At her new home in the land of Judah, Ruth worked during the harvest season to feed her mother-in-law and herself. In a farmer's field, she gathered leftover grain that the harvesters dropped. The owner of the field, Boaz, noticed Ruth working. Hearing from his men that she took care of his relative Naomi like a daughter cares for a mother, Boaz invited Ruth to remain in his field for the duration of the harvest, where she would be safe and have plenty of grain to gather.

> "At this, she bowed down with her face to the ground. She exclaimed, 'Why have I found such favor in your eyes that you notice me—a foreigner?'" (Ruth 2:10).

Ruth was overwhelmed with gratitude. She was thankful to Boaz, and almost certainly thankful to God. She immediately responded to God's blessing with worship. Perhaps she didn't know God well yet or have a close relationship with Him, perhaps she didn't understand everything yet, but she could worship.

We can have the same response: I am not in the best situation right now, but I can worship. I can find God in the little blessings.

Once you begin to worship, things become clearer, and your mission becomes more empowered.

3. Turn right at obedience.

"One day Naomi her mother-in-law said to her, 'My daughter, should I not try to find a home for you, where you will be well provided for? Is not Boaz, with whose servant girls you have been, a kinsman of ours? Tonight he will be winnowing barley on the threshing floor. Wash and perfume yourself, and put on your best clothes. Then go down to the threshing floor, but don't let him know you are there until he has finished eating and drinking. When he lies down, note the place where he is lying. Then go and uncover his feet and lie down. He will tell you what to do.'

'I will do whatever you say,' Ruth answered" (Ruth 3:1-5).

Sound a little odd? It sounded odd to Ruth too. You want me to do *what*?

Ruth was a virtuous woman, and she hadn't hooked up with any of the young men who were workers in the field. Boaz knew this. Everybody knew this. And Naomi asked her to do something that seemed a little awkward, to say the least.

Ruth didn't know how the whole kinsmen redeemer thing worked. She wasn't aware of the custom and what all it entailed. She just obeyed. She had the right spirit and the right heart.

When we have the right spirit and the right heart, God blesses and empowers us as well.

We often think that we have to understand before we obey. That's getting the cart in front of the horse. We obey and then we begin to understand.

For example, raising kids. Sometimes we know they don't understand why we're requiring them to do a certain thing, but we just try to teach them to obey: You may not understand, but you must obey.

If we obey, then the understanding will come.

Even when we don't understand the tragedies and turns in life, we just obey. When we stay on course, we will understand better, by and by.

Ruth lost her husband, her father-in-law, brother-in-law, said good-bye forever to her sister-in-law, and finally left her homeland behind. She committed herself to stay with Naomi and to worship Naomi's God. Then she worshiped that God and obeyed where His inspirations led. In the end, she married Boaz and became an ancestor of Jesus.

God empowered her mission. He empowers ours when we do the same—when we jumper-cable our spiritual batteries onto God.

A NASA engineer, during his night off, considered a work of science fiction that had originated in the creative mind of a novelist. When a similar tragedy struck the Apollo 13 crew later that same night, the fictional scene inspired a solution to power the batteries of the real command module, *Odyssey*. For the engineering team at Mission Control, hope became mission *possible*.

Committed to their journey, their mission became empowered. The engineers developed a battery plan to transfer a battery charge from the lunar module battery system to that in the command module, via something like jumper cables. The plan would enable safe reentry through Earth's atmosphere for real-life astronauts Lovell, Swigert, and Haise.

Apollo 13, miracle number seven.

Faith Accelerator

List any "impossible" blessings God has given you *or* miracles you have heard about from trusted sources.

How have these miracles charged your faith and your hope in God's living, active presence in your day-to-day life? After each "impossible" blessing or miracle, write your answers.

Finally, pray that God empowers your faith, hope, and actions as you carry out the unique mission He handpicked for you.

*An inflight photo of the improvised oxygen filter and duct tape
constructed and used aboard Apollo 13.
Credit: NASA.*

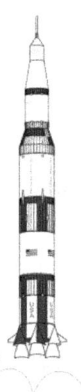

Chapter 8
Sticky Situations

Apollo 13 Miracle #8: Duct Tape

Lovell, Swigert, and Haise's troubles were far from over.

The lunar module, which the astronauts were now using as a lifeboat, had been designed to sustain two astronauts as they conducted a two-day mission on the surface of the moon. The LM had not been designed to support three men while they traveled around the moon and back to Earth over a period of four or more days.

The carbon dioxide (CO_2) filters of the LM could not continue to filter the breathing oxygen. The men's own exhalations now set off alarms and began to threaten their lives.

Within twenty-four hours the Apollo Mission Operations Team from the Mission Evaluation Room (MER)—sometimes called the "MER-men"—would have to develop a solution.

Attempting a never-before-devised filtration assembly using assorted items the astronauts had on board—including spacesuit hosing, moon rock bags, bungee cords, cardboard, and square command module air filters that couldn't fit the round lunar module filtration unit—the MER-men provided the astronauts an odd construction procedure for a possible fix.

The most important part of the procedure? Lovell, Swigert, and Haise would need to seal the improvised system's leaks and joints with duct tape, which NASA had placed on board spacecraft since the days of the Gemini missions—just in case.

After an hour of construction time, the astronauts attached the cobbled-together, duct-taped oxygen filtration system and activated it. As the nation and people around the world prayed for Apollo 13's astronauts, the dangerous lunar module CO_2 levels began to fall, and breathing grew easier for the crew. The duct-taped contraption worked!

Undoubtedly, so did the prayers. Woodfill said, "It seems nostalgic to reflect on . . . a time when America saw the value of prayer from the leadership down to the brilliant minds that were directing the space program. No doubt, God gave us favor during those days of unprecedented success because of our dependence on Him." He stated emphatically, "God had made a way of fitting a square peg into a round hole because the nation prayed that Tuesday evening in April of 1970. When the Master Engineer of the Universe, the Lord Jesus Christ, [is] called as a problem solver, He never fails."

"I urge, then, first of all, that requests, prayers, intercession and thanksgiving be made for everyone . . ." (1 Timothy 2:1).

Woodfill showed the depth of his trust in God when he said, "The Bible speaks of God knowing the number of hairs on our heads. The average number of hair follicles at any one time on a person is 100,000. Each hair follicle can grow about 20 hairs in a person's lifetime. So God knows about 2,000,000 of our hairs.

"Now the number of parts in the command module was about 2,000,000. Isn't it reasonable to conclude that God knows each of those parts as well as our hairs? But He cares much more about the men on board than their hair, so . . . He can impart wisdom to fix any of those millions of parts to make that . . . work."

I can't help but smile when I read those words. Many of these engineers were committed to a space program that they saw as bringing glory to God, not to men.

Man's Spiritual "Duct Tape": Stick Relentlessly with God

Though you and I may not have gone into space and had our lives threatened in the way the three astronauts did, we've all experienced times of extreme, perhaps almost unbearable, stress.

In those situations, we can succumb to the pressure of the adverse environment we're in, or we can find a way to make the situation work. We can be immobilized with fear and uncertainty, or we can find a way, regardless of how unconventional it may be, to survive *and* to thrive.

Consider 2 Samuel 5, as David and his men approached Jerusalem and its massive walls. The city inhabitants were so confident of their ability to defend themselves against David's army, they cried out, *"'You will not get in here; even the blind and the lame can ward you off.' They thought, 'David cannot get in here'" (2 Samuel 5:6b).*

David gathered his men together and said, "We'll attack through the water shaft" (2 Samuel 5:8). Soon after, Jerusalem became called the City of David.

The old adage says, "Where there is a will, there is a way." Someone modified it with this change, "Where there is a bill, there is a way." Regardless of how you say it, since the beginning of time the determination of man to accomplish, to break all barriers, to find a way, is well documented. The force of strength, the ingenuity, the endurance of humanity against all odds still amazes us.

This aspect of our nature is not limited to physical matters only. It is also possible to take that same determination and use it in spiritual matters. We know from the Word of God that there are at least three ways to get the favor and attention of God during a crisis.

1. Relentless Pursuit

The motto for Lexus, the luxury carmaker, is "The relentless pursuit of perfection." Not just pursuit, but the relentless pursuit. There is something inspiring about people who will not quit until they get what they're going for. God responds positively to relentless pursuit.

In the New Testament, Mark 2 reveals the story of a young man who was paralyzed and confined to a bed. The young man, along with four of his friends, heard that Jesus had arrived in town. They decided immediately to go to Jesus for a healing. Unfortunately, crowds became so large around Jesus that the four men couldn't get their paralyzed friend through to Him.

Jesus was teaching and healing the needs of the people inside a house. The four men who carried their friend on a stretcher or cot couldn't budge the crowd. Rather than be discouraged and quit trying, the young men brainstormed an idea. They carried their friend up to the roof of the house. They took the roof apart until there was a big enough hole to lower their paralyzed friend down to the feet of Jesus.

I can only imagine the expressions of the crowd as these young men tore up the roof of someone's house. But Jesus didn't disapprove of their actions. In fact, He honored them. He saw their desire, and their relentless pursuit. Jesus healed the crippled friend and forgave his sins.

Jesus honors pursuit—finding a way to solve a problem that God would acknowledge as important to solve. It seems crazy, but God responds to gatecrashers. Maybe because Jesus Himself was a gatecrasher.

"As [Jesus] approached the town gate, a dead person was being carried out—the only son of his mother, and she was a

widow. And a large crowd from the town was with her. When the Lord saw her, His heart went out to her and He said, 'Don't cry.'

Then He went up and touched the coffin, and those carrying it stood still. He said, 'Young man, I say to you, get up!' The dead man sat up and began to talk, and Jesus gave him back to his mother" (Luke 7:12-15).

The Lord was a gatecrasher. He decided to go to a funeral that He hadn't been invited to. He stopped the service and raised the boy up out of his box.

Jesus also invited Himself to people's houses. In Luke 19, a publican (a Jew who collected taxes from the Jews for the Romans) named Zacchaeus hid in a Sycamore tree. He'd wanted to see Jesus coming down the road, but hadn't wanted anyone to see him. Jesus stopped walking right under the tree and told the man, "Zacchaeus, we're going to eat at your house today" (Luke 19:5).

Even angels are gatecrashers. In Acts 12 when Peter was locked in an inner prison, God sent a gatecrashing angel to bust him loose. The angel woke Peter, and Peter's chains fell off his arms. Then the angel told Peter to follow him out.

> **NASA Trivia:** Which astronaut recently penned the words, "Mars has been flown by, orbited, smacked into, radar examined, and rocketed onto, as well as bounced upon, rolled over, shoveled, drilled into, baked, and even blasted. Still to come: Mars being stepped on"?[9]
> *(See footnote for answer.)*

A gatecrasher is anyone who will pursue what they desire without reservation. They will not take no for an answer. They will not stop until they accomplish their mission. In the world of faith,

---

[9] Buzz Aldrin, in his 2013 book *Mission to Mars: My Vision for Space Exploration*.

we must storm the gates of hell if needed in order to stick with God. We must not be timid or afraid.

When it comes to your soul, you have to pursue an ever-increasing faith. Many people don't pursue God because they don't want to be rude or impolite. When it comes to your soul, you have to pursue. The enemy wants to plant thoughts in your mind, especially after a setback, that you're not valuable anymore, or that you're no longer wanted in your church. "You don't belong there. You don't fit in. Those people will not let you in the club. They are just too good or too holy to handle someone like you. It would be best for you to stay home. It would be best for you to stay away."

A spiritual gatecrasher who sticks with God will not let the enemy, or anyone else, keep them in a state of paralysis. You have to make up your mind that no mistake, no mishap, no emotional heartache or loss is going to keep you away from the presence of God. You have to make up your mind to pursue even when it is hard just to move.

When you pursue relentlessly though you don't emotionally feel God's presence, then you are pushing.

2. Push

The Bible tells us about a little lady with a chronic disease. She spent all her money trying to find a cure through the doctors of the day. They had been unsuccessful. She decided to try and get to Jesus, but the crowd was so large she couldn't get near Him. She was sick and weak, but she decided to push.

So she began to push and fight her way through the crowd. She only wanted to touch Jesus, perhaps even just His clothes, and believed she would be healed. When she finally touched His robe, she was healed instantly. The supernatural healing energy went out of Jesus and into her sick body when her need made contact with His power (Mark 5:25-34).

Jesus responds to people who push to reach Him. He responds to people who push through all the voices of doubt and fear. Jesus wants us to push past all the people who say, "You'll never be the same. You can never recover or return. You've done too much or gone too far."

We have to push past the naysayers. We have to find a way to get back to and stick with God.

The Bible tells us in the Old Testament about four lepers who were made to stay outside the city limits. The city of Samaria had banned them because of their highly contagious leprosy. So the four stayed out by the city dump, waiting to die. The Syrian army had surrounded the city and was not allowing any food to go in to Samaria. The city of Samaria was starving to death because of this blockade. The four lepers had a decision to make: 1) They could sit where they were and die, 2) they could go into the city of Samaria where people were already starting to die, or 3) they could charge the most powerful army in the world, the Syrian army, and hope for victory.

The latter seemed like a suicide mission, but they were really out of choices. The lepers made a decision to go to the Syrian camp. God rewarded them. When they got to the camp, it was full of food and the army was gone. God had sent a loud sound in the night that caused the Syrian army so much fear that they ran and left everything behind. The lepers enjoyed a feast (2 Kings 7:8).

I can't recall a single example in the Bible of when the Lord told a faith-driven gatecrasher to get out. If they had a need and were willing to push, it was always followed by victory. If they had a spiritual or other deep need, God found a way to get them past the barriers.

Why don't more people push to get into the favor of God? I believe it's because we feel outmatched by our enemy. In physical matters, we have confidence in our strength, but in spiritual matters, we feel we're out of our league, so we don't relentlessly pursue or push. We try to find a way, but if it's a little too difficult, we figure "it's not the will of God."

It's always the will of God for us to accomplish the mission God has chosen for us. In our own strength we are outmatched, but with God on our side, we are never outmatched.

3. Persevere

For push to be successful, you have to push for a continued period of time. This type of push is called perseverance. It is the prevailing determination of the soul regardless of obstacles and difficulties.

"If God is for us, who can be against us?" (Romans 8:31b).

Spiritual perseverance is a combination of your pursuit and God's power.

*"'Ask and it **will** be given to you; seek and you **will** find; knock and the door **will** be opened to you'" (Matthew 7:7; emphasis added).*

Like blind Bartimaeus. He was kept behind the crowds and told to be quiet, but his calls to Jesus grew louder and louder. *". . . He began to shout, 'Jesus, Son of David, have mercy on me!'" (Mark 10:47b)* until Jesus heard him. When Jesus heard his cry, He stopped everything and healed the man.

Perseverance requires getting stronger in your pursuit when adversity gets stronger in its attempt to hinder you.

The engineers, technicians, and all the support people at Mission Control could not get discouraged, though obstacles mounted by the second. They had to persevere through every setback. They had to stay focused on the goal.

Jesus gave an example of a widow and an unjust judge. The judge said her petition was granted because she kept coming back, persisting, in her quest for justice. Then Jesus said, *"'And will not God bring about justice for His chosen ones, who cry out to Him day and night? Will He keep putting them off?'" (Luke 18:7).*

Politeness will not grant you your petition, but persistence will. It may take crashing the gate with relentless pursuit, pushing, and persisting, but God never turns away a faith-driven person. He loves us, infinitely and immeasurably.

Paul was right when he concluded Romans 8 with powerful words of persistence.

"For I am convinced that neither death nor life, neither angels nor demons, neither the present nor the future, nor any powers, neither height nor depth, nor anything else in all creation, will be able to separate us from the love of God that is in Christ Jesus our Lord" (Romans 8:38-39).

That conviction is spiritual duct tape.

You thought you were finished, but God gave you another chance. The enemy thought you were finished, but you got back up again. The enemy kept knocking you down, but you kept standing to your feet. Recovery is the result of repeated renewal through Bible study and prayer. I'm bruised, I'm battered, but I'm back.

A man in our church was discouraged because he kept falling back into the same mistakes. I told him, "It's not a question of how many times you fall. It's only a question of how many times you get back up. You only have to get back up one more time than you fell."

Make every effort to keep standing up, and to continue sticking with God.

Because the engineers at Mission Control relentlessly pursued and pushed, they persevered in developing a never-before conceived life-sustaining contraption. For Lovell, Swigert, and Haise, survival would have been difficult, if not impossible, without the inventive CO_2 filtration system . . . secured by sticky duct tape.

Apollo 13, miracle number eight.

FAITH ACCELERATOR

List the times you relentlessly pursued, pushed, and persisted to receive an answer or blessing from God, and He provided the answer or blessing—no matter how "odd looking" His system of blessing may have seemed.

For example, years ago God "blessed" one of my editors with kidney failure in order to get her out of a dangerous situation and save her life. She has since received an organ transplant. Through this, God twice blessed her determination to trust and "stick with" Him.

In the future when you find yourself in an overwhelming, stressful situation, reread your written entries. Then relentlessly pursue, push, and persist in prayer, trusting in God's proven ability, love, and willingness to save.

_____
_____
_____
_____
_____
_____
_____
_____
_____
_____
_____
_____
_____
_____
_____
_____
_____

View of Earth's terminator. Credit: NASA.

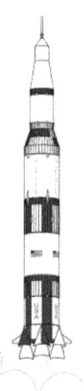

Chapter 9
Guidance System

Apollo 13 Miracle #9: A Navigation Mishap

As the spacecraft moved in the direction of Earth, the astronauts had clean, filtered oxygen to breathe. Unfortunately, challenges continued to plague Mission Control. Most notably, keeping Apollo 13 on trajectory for reentry.

Rather than reenter, Apollo 13's current trajectory would cause the ship to skip off Earth's atmosphere and into space. Without course correction, the crew would perish.

To make matters worse, due to the explosion and the critical need to save every volt and amp of battery power for reentry procedures, the guidance computers were shut down, unavailable. And, surrounded by a cloud of glittering metallic debris from the blast, the astronauts couldn't distinguish the sun and stars to navigate.

Coincidently or not, one NASA astronaut had faced a similar situation once before. It had been during his flight aboard Apollo 8 just over a year earlier.

Coincidently or not, that astronaut was Jim Lovell.

Some time prior to Apollo 8, a forward-thinking employee of the contractor TRW, which helped design navigational systems for

NASA, had considered a backup plan in the event a spacecraft were unable to navigate by the stars. His idea? Navigate using Earth's terminator—the shadow/sunlight line from North Pole to South Pole where darkness terminates and daylight begins.

The employee worked the geometry and created a computer program to test it. The technique was validated and approved for use at Mission Control.

On Apollo 8, Jim Lovell served as navigator during the first-ever manned lunar orbit. Near the end of the orbit as he prepared to return to Earth, Lovell worked at the navigation computer and entered the coordinates. Then, inadvertently, he pressed the CLR (clear) key rather than the ENTR key beside it. The coordinates vanished. At Mission Control, someone recalled the backup navigation plan that would use Earth's terminator in lieu of the guidance computer. They decided to try the backup "seat-of-pants" navigation method. It worked, smooth as a polished sextant.

Now, surrounded by a cloud of twinkling debris, Lovell's Apollo 8 mishap and subsequent test of the backup navigation method seemed like a God-send. Lovell, Swigert, and Haise would be able to adjust course using Earth's terminator while they performed another lunar module engine burn. No electricity would be needed.

The procedure was a success . . . because God had allowed a previous setback aboard Apollo 8, and because the Apollo 13 crew had focused on a clear, fixed point.

Successful Navigation through Life

The navigation of your life on this Earth will only work if you have a fixed point.

A fellow attorney friend of mine told me that the biggest difference between us was that I believed everything in the Bible was true. He didn't.

I said, "Fair enough. Then what is your fixed point?"

"Fixed point?" he asked. "What do you mean?"

I explained, "Everybody uses something to steer their life by. Just as a compass needs the fixed point of 'north' to determine all other directions, we measure our decisions and choices based on a fixed point of some reliable source." I continued, "For me that is the Bible. I measure social norms and behavior based on that fixed point. What is your fixed point? What is the line that you navigate by?"

He thought for a moment. "I suppose it would be my own experiences, understanding, and feelings."

I replied, "With all due respect, that's pretty flimsy, because as humans we're not really objective witnesses. We are not reliable resources. We're emotional. We're volatile. We change. If we have a wind blowing against us, like someone criticizing us, we don't always respond correctly or accurately. If law school taught us anything, it taught us that a subjective standard is not as reliable as an objective standard." I attempted to find common ground with the law. "Our interpretation is subjective, but a written report, statute, law, or Bible is an objective standard."

He consented and said he needed a more reliable fixed point.

The writer of Psalm 112 described a man who feared God and kept God's commands. The psalmist said that that man would not be afraid of bad news or trouble because his heart was steadfast—fixed—on God. The word "fixed" here isn't referring to a repair but rather a steady position. A terminator line.

If you keep the commandments of the Lord and have a healthy respect for the consequences of not doing so, then you have a "fixed point." If you have a fixed point, you can navigate even when debris surrounds you and junk flies at you. Your surroundings appear chaotic, but the line is fixed.

This fixed point gives you more than just clarity of judgment and stability. It also gives you a sense of protection and security. Inherently, we understand that if our lives are based on the Word, we are on solid ground. Our humanity is well aware of its frailty, but with a fixed point, we react with confidence and strength.

Recently, a student at a local college wanted to interview me for a paper she was doing at her school concerning faith in America. She taped the interview on camera with the intention of showing it to her class when she presented her paper.

The student asked several questions that were thoughtful but finally came to the question of all questions for a Christian: "How do you convince someone to follow Jesus if they don't believe in the Word of God?"

I responded, "There are historical, literary, and archeological references to the life of Jesus. But it is one thing to know He lived; it is another to follow Him." I then explained, "Believing in the Word of God is more reliable than any other source of subjective standards, but ultimately it is a question of faith." I can use a sextant to navigate based on the fixed points of stars and planets, but I have to believe that God is the Creator of those stars.

I concluded my interview with the student by stating, "Faith is not an unreliable source. In fact, it takes more faith to believe in the big bang theory or evolution than it does to believe in creationism. We all believe something. We all have a fixed point. My fixed point has the legitimacy of 6000 years of history."

The problem with a storm is that it disorients you. It gives you spiritual vertigo. You don't know which way is up or down. When that happens, you have to trust your instruments (God's faithfulness, His promises in the Bible) and not your doubt. You have to trust the objective standard and ignore the subjective standard.

A Line to Divide Darkness and Light

The engineers who worked at the Johnson and Kennedy Space Centers in the Apollo program became more convinced than ever that there is a Creator who established the universe and put everything in motion. The reason was that all of their mathematical calculations about positioning their spacecraft in orbits and on the moon were based on the consistency of the heavens.

The fixed point that the Apollo 13 astronauts navigated by was a line that divided the light from the darkness. God had a dividing line from the beginning. Creation was established with dividing lines. A line determines the separation between two clearly defined substances. Two clearly defined choices. Two clearly defined lifestyles.

"And God said, 'Let there be light,' and there was light. God saw that the light was good, and He separated the light from the darkness" (Genesis 1:3-4).

We live in a world of pluralistic views of God. But God is singular; He is not pluralistic.

"Hear, O Israel: The Lord our God, the Lord is one" (Deuteronomy 6:4).

". . . One Lord, one faith, one baptism; one God and Father of all, who is over all and through all and in all" (Ephesians 4:5-6).

God clearly divides what is right and what is wrong. He is not confused about the light and the darkness.

We would do well to get a revelation of the strength in drawing a line, and then live life based on that boundary. We get into trouble when we don't place a boundary between light and darkness. We think God is okay with everything running together. Not so! The line that God draws is not a dotted line or a perforated line. It is a fixed line, one that isn't going to change with human fads or customs.

"Then the Lord answered Job out of the storm. He said:
'Who is this that darkens My counsel
with words without knowledge?

Brace yourself like a man;
I will question you,
and you shall answer Me.
Where were you when I laid the earth's foundation?
Tell Me, if you understand.
Who marked off its dimensions? Surely you know!
*Who stretched a measuring **line across it**?'"*
(Job 38:1-5; emphasis added).

> **NASA Trivia:** Where is the famous white vest that Gene Kranz wore during the Apollo 13 mission?[10]
>
> *(See footnote for answer.)*

A Line to Divide Death and Life

A dividing line exists between life and death. If you keep to one side, you are alive. If you step to the other side, you are not.

Several years ago while studying in Dublin, Ireland, I visited Belfast, North Ireland. The entire city brimmed with steel-plated Humvee-type war vehicles. They monitored the streets—a war zone where fear dominated every corner.

A dividing line ran through Belfast. At sunset the gates closed, dividing the city in half. If you got caught on the wrong side, your life was in danger until morning when the gates opened and you could make it safely back to your side. Life and death was determined by a measuring line.

---

[10] Today Gene Kranz's vest is a pride of the Smithsonian National Air and Space Museum.

"David also defeated the Moabites. He made them lie down on the ground and measured them off with a length of cord. Every two lengths of them were put to death, and the third length was allowed to live. So the Moabites became subject to David and brought tribute" (2 Samuel 8:2).

"The men said to her, 'This oath you made us swear will not be binding on us unless, when we enter the land, you have tied this scarlet cord in the window . . .'" (Joshua 2:17-18a).

What lines do (or will) you put in your life? What is fixed? What is nonnegotiable? What is your default position? May the scarlet line of the blood of Jesus guide your every decision and choice!

"The man brought me back to the entrance of the temple, and I saw water coming out from under the threshold of the temple toward the east (for the temple faced east). The water was coming down from under the south side of the temple, south of the altar. He then brought me out through the north gate and led me around the outside to the outer gate facing east, and the water was flowing from the south side.

As the man went eastward with a measuring line in his hand, he measured off a thousand cubits and then led me through water that was ankle-deep. He measured off another thousand cubits and led me through water that was knee-deep. He measured off another thousand and led me through water that was up to the waist. He measured off another thousand, but now it was a river that I could not cross, because the water had risen and was deep enough to swim in—a river that no one could cross" (Ezekiel 47:1-5).

Old Testament prophet Ezekiel tells of a man he saw who had a line in his hand. A representative of a God who measured. A God who created a precise world. So precise, we can navigate by it.

The space program has done it for years in the extraterrestrial world, and sailors at sea before that, but mankind has been navigating God's world spiritually for millennia. We can continue to count on His guidance as we navigate it now, because He created it.

God used a navigational mishap aboard Apollo 8 to bring about a life-saving course correction for three stalwart astronauts, now headed toward Earth, with the terminator line that God created leading them.

Apollo 13, miracle number nine.

FAITH ACCELERATOR

Write thoughts this chapter inspired that will help you to successfully navigate through trials and temptations. What trials and temptations do you currently or often face? What terminator line or lines can you put in place to help you clearly see right from wrong? Use this, as well as prayer and God's guidance, to steer away from troubles and toward safety.

_____
_____
_____
_____
_____
_____
_____
_____
_____

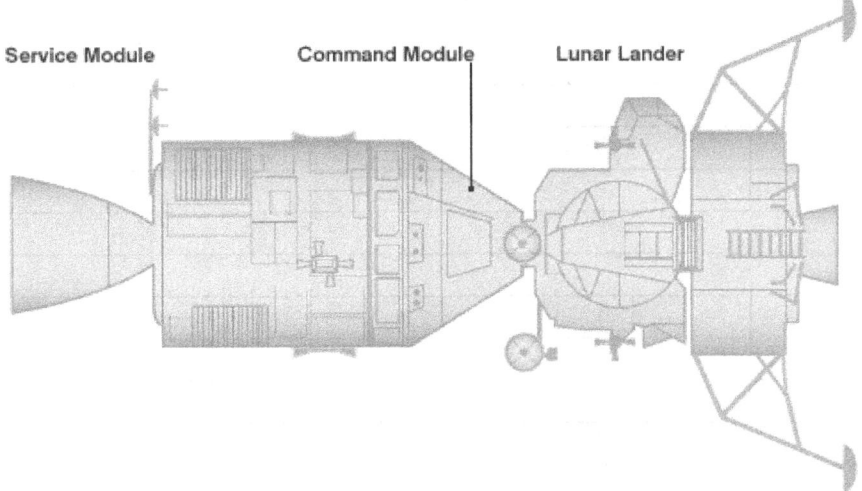

Diagram of the Apollo 13 service module, command module ("capsule"), and lunar module (L to R). The round hatch is visible between the command and lunar modules. Credit: NASA.

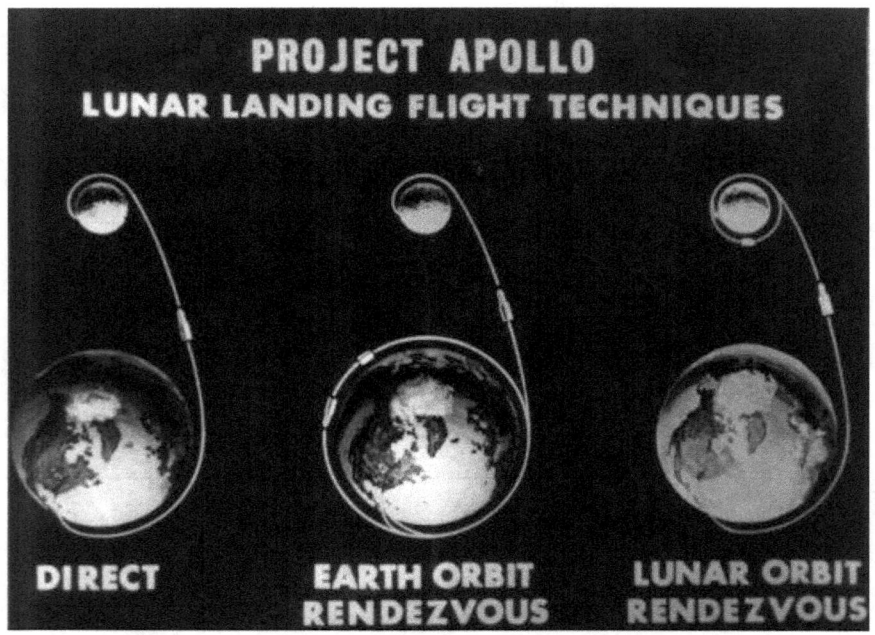

The three different Apollo flight modes. Credit: NASA

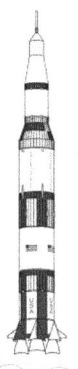

Chapter 10
The Heavenly Rendezvous Approach

Apollo 13 Miracle #10: The Functioning Hatch

When the April 13th explosion rocked the spacecraft, Jim Lovell, thinking the lunar module may have been struck and breached by a meteor, had told Swigert to close—"button up"—the hatch between the command module and the LM, so they wouldn't depressurize.

Both Swigert and Lovell had worked to seal it, but the hatch would not stay shut. After five tries between them, they still couldn't get it to latch. Realizing they hadn't been breached since the pressure remained constant, they had set the hatch to the side.

Fortunately—virtually miraculously, according to engineer Jerry Woodfill—the open hatch had enabled the astronauts to save moments of critical time in transferring to and powering up LM lifeboat.

Now the astronauts were back in the command module, finally nearing Earth's atmosphere and preparing for reentry. Because they would soon need to jettison the LM, they would have to find some way to force the hatch to seal.

Amazingly, no force was needed. When they tried to close it, it slipped smoothly into place, and latched.

The Power of *Again*

The uniqueness of believing in Jesus Christ is *resurrection power*. The disciplines of various faiths resonate with different cultures. All of them focus on a life that supposedly benefits from philosophical guidance.

The question that remains in each faith that is *not* Christ centered is, "What do I do when my world falls apart?" Subscribing to a series of self-help books doesn't help when my self has been ravaged by rampant sin.

Where is the reset button of Islam? It is couched in martyrdom.

Where is the resurrection of the Bahia's faith? It is centered on utopian communities.

Where is the resurrection of Hinduism, Judaism, and Shintoism? They are all belief mechanisms that subscribe to rigorous rituals without a resurrection.

Buddhism and Jainism have no resurrection power.

There is only one who rose from the dead. His name is Jesus.

This resurrection is more than just bragging rights. It is more than just my God is bigger than your god. This resurrection power permeates the very DNA of our faith. It is a power that recreates. Therefore, we not only serve the *C*reator, we serve the one who recreates, restores, renews, returns, revives, and replenishes.

The prefix "re" simply means *again*.

At the heart of resurrection is again. First we had life, and now we have life again.

Is there anybody better equipped to give us life again than the one who gave us life initially? If I have a Sears washing machine that breaks, I take it back to Sears; I don't take it to Wal-Mart. Who better to fix a product than the people who manufactured it? Who better to save my soul than the one who made my soul? Who better to give me a new start than the one who gave me a start to begin with?

Who better to fix the Apollo 13 hatch than the One who allowed it to malfunction in the first place?

Sin has the ability to dismantle an individual because of its constant, relentless nature. It doesn't knock once and leave. It is a persistent stranger. An ongoing malfunction outside the will of God. The continual attack of our enemy wears us down. An attack can be subtle, but if it's constant it can wear down anyone or anything.

I've watched small puddles of water develop in coastal shorelines where massive boulders and rocks are shaped by a tide that splashes and then drifts back. The continual coming of water does more than just neutralize the strength of a rock. It reshapes it. It reforms it. It creates holes and forms caverns. Sin has a similar personality. It keeps on coming. It keeps on driving.

Fortunately the Bible tells us, *". . . Where sin increased, grace increased all the more . . ." (Romans 5:20b).* How do we gain a superior position? We must have the power of again—resurrection power.

"Resurrection," by the way, comes from the Latin *surgere* (to rise or to surge) and *re-* (again). To rise up or surge again.

When Jesus healed people's leprosy, He reversed the destructive deterioration of the disease. The slow death was reversed. Now, instead of deterioration, there was restoration.

The prefix "de" means *to remove or separate from*. This is what sin does. It separates us from our Creator.

But God, through His resurrection power, reconnects us by renewing our minds and restoring our bodies. He returns us again to the place of fellowship with God. Nobody but Jesus can do this, because nobody else has resurrection power. He alone returned—raised Himself—from the dead!

If you don't have resurrection power, you don't stand a chance against sin. You can't help yourself or anybody else.

"I want to know Christ and the power of His resurrection and the fellowship of sharing in His sufferings, becoming like Him in His death, and so, somehow, to attain to the resurrection from the dead" (Philippians 3:10-11).

In 2 Kings 5, a man called Naaman was the commander of the Syrian army—the most powerful army in the world at that time. Naaman also had leprosy. An Israelite maid in his household told his wife that Elisha, a prophet in Israel, could save his life.

Naaman went to Elisha's house. Instead of meeting with Naaman, Elisha sent a servant to him with a message: *"Go, wash yourself seven times in the Jordan, and your flesh will be restored and you will be cleansed"* (2 Kings 5:10b).

Rather than be impressed that Elisha had somehow known that he had arrived and why, Naaman was mad. He had expected the royal welcome and wanted to be fussed over amid a flourish of hands and the equivalent of magic words. He prepared to climb into his chariot and have his driver head the rig back to Syria.

However, Naaman's servant talked him into giving Elisha's method a try, and so Naaman went to the river. The muddy Jordan River.

I can almost envision the scene and hear the conversation between the servant and Naaman as he dunked himself in the Jordan River, holding his nose.

Naaman: "That's once."
Servant: "Go again."
Naaman: (*Sighs.*) "Twice . . . that has to be enough."
Servant: "Do it again."
Naaman: "That's three times. Nothing is happening!"
Servant: "Do it again. . . ."

If you have a faith need, don't stop until you get it met. Only God can make things brand new again. "I need the Holy Spirit, and I asked God, but nothing happened." Ask again.

After Naaman dunked the seventh time, his *"flesh was restored and became clean like that of a young boy" (2 Kings 5:14b).*

Only God can return a person or thing to its original state or renew it. Only God can restore a spacecraft hatch that previously didn't work.

Resurrection power begins with God and is transferred to His people. Power to restore. Power to heal. Power to save. That's the power of again. That's the power of return. The power of resurrection faith.

In his book *David and Goliath*, author Malcolm Gladwell makes the case that only legitimate power produces the right results. Power that is not legitimate does not create an atmosphere of compliance and submission. It creates an atmosphere of defiance and anarchy.

The reason that death, sickness, and suffering are compliant and submissive to Jesus, and ultimately to us through the Holy Spirit, is that inherently even diseases know that the power of Jesus' resurrection is legitimate.

Gladwell concludes his book by saying, "If you take away a mother or a father, you cause suffering and despair, but one time in ten, out of that despair rises an indomitable force. You see the giant and the shepherd in the Valley of Elah and your eye is drawn to the man with the sword and the shield and the glittering armor. But so much of what is beautiful and valuable in the world comes from the shepherd, who has more strength and purpose than we ever imagined."

That strength and purpose comes to any human who learns how to trust God. Trust His resurrection power to return you again to a place of wholeness . . . just as He restored the hatch that enabled the Apollo 13 astronauts to return safely home.

The Strongest Connection

In the early 1950s, people thought going to the moon was science fiction. But by the late 1950s, we were earnestly trying to make it a reality, and were racing the Soviet Union. The German scientist who assisted us, Wernher von Braun, became known as the father of space travel.

By 1961, different ideas emerged from various think tanks as to how we might accomplish the goal of landing on the moon.

These thinkers settled on three possibilities.

1. **The direct-ascent approach.** A giant rocket with thirty engines would fly directly to the moon.
2. **The Earth-orbital rendezvous.** Two rockets would get man to the moon: one to blast off carrying the crew, and a second in orbit with additional propellant, where the spacecraft could refuel for the remaining trip to the moon.
3. **The lunar orbit rendezvous.** A three-stage Saturn rocket booster, plus a two-part Apollo vehicle: 1) a command and service module, and 2) a lunar module. The two-part vehicle would travel together, connected, to the moon. In lunar orbit they would separate, and the lunar lander alone would descend to the moon's surface. Afterward it would ascend again and reconnect to the command and service module for the trip home.

After much debate, the decision was made to use the third option, the lunar orbit rendezvous system.

Meanwhile, the Soviets were well underway with the direct-ascent approach using a single Nova style rocket with thirty engines and more than twelve million pounds of thrust. This seemed like the best and fastest way to get there, and the Soviets were as eager as the United States to win the race.

But the Bible says, *". . . The race is not to the swift . . ."* *(Ecclesiastes 9:11b).*

Twice in 1969, once just a week before our Apollo 11 launch, the Soviets' rockets exploded on the launch pad. Of the thirty engines, only one rocket had to malfunction for the entire cluster to fail. Their cosmonauts died in the process, heroic and not forgotten.

Fast forward now to Apollo 13 and 1970. We've been to the moon twice. In addition, the fact that NASA's design included a lunar module enabled the crew to take refuge in that module as a lifeboat in space.

One system killed cosmonauts and failed. Another system saved astronauts and twice landed on the moon. The significant difference: Our system required us to rendezvous with the heavenly, to rendezvous with God's orbit in space. This approach was based on God's creation and order, and not just man's created machine. We tied in to what God already had in place, piggybacking on His plan and perfection, instead of trying to blast our way there.

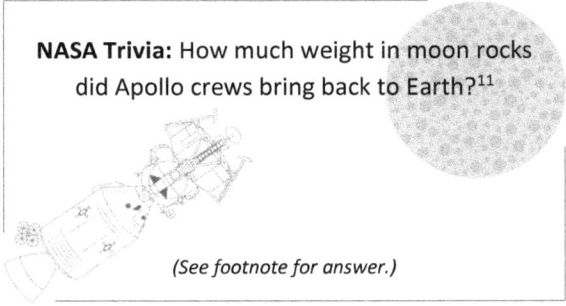

NASA Trivia: How much weight in moon rocks did Apollo crews bring back to Earth?[11]

(See footnote for answer.)

The birth of Jesus is a similar approach, though moving in the opposite direction. God decided to rendezvous with humanity, not by blasting here from heaven, but by connecting with mankind through a virgin birth. Jesus was the Son of God. God manifest in the flesh. God with us. God took on human form and was born in a

---

[11] The six Apollo lunar missions (Apollos 11, 12, 14, 15, 16, and 17) returned with a total of 842 pounds of dust and rock.

barn, a stable for animals. If ever we can see deity lowering itself to connect with humanity, it is in the birth of Christ in Bethlehem.

There are different approaches to how we can live life. One approach is to do it all by yourself. We can live an independent life based on a humanistic philosophy—a belief that God is only a figment of man's imagination, and that man's mind is the highest Supreme Being.

The alternative is to rendezvous with what God is doing, to decide that you are going to do things God's way. You're going to live your life based on what heaven is doing rather than what humanity is doing.

To accomplish this, here are three ways that you can connect to Him.

1. Connect with His Word.

This is what God did when He was made manifest in flesh.

". . . Faith comes from hearing the message, and the message is heard through the word of Christ" (Romans 10:17).

It is that connection with the Word that changes us from the inside out. God speaks to us through the Bible.

2. Connect with His ways.

The Bible says that His ways and thoughts are higher than ours (Isaiah 55:9), and yet we can connect. We can rendezvous!

"Your attitude should be the same as that of Christ Jesus . . ." (Philippians 2:5).

We have to connect with His ways, and that means showing love to people the way Jesus did, imitating Him. Our human flesh says it's better to receive than to give, but God says it's better to give than receive (Acts 20:35). Real joy comes from having that understanding and connecting to it in a tangible way.

"Let us not become weary in doing good, for at the proper time we will reap a harvest if we do not give up. Therefore, as we

have opportunity, let us do good to all people, especially to those who belong to the family of believers" (Galatians 6:9-10).

3. Connect with His will.

You never know what explosions are going to happen in life. It's important to be able to crawl up in the cocoon of God's will and take refuge. You can't do that if you're trying to do things your way or on your own. John the Baptist said, *"He must become greater; I must become less." (John 3:30).*

What is God's will? The Bible reveals His will for your life.

"The Lord is not slow in keeping His promise, as some understand slowness. He is patient with you, not wanting anyone to perish, but everyone to come to repentance" (2 Peter 3:9).

It is not God's will that you or I, or anyone else, would perish, nor that we live lives focused primarily on ourselves. It's His will that everyone, in spite of any setback, be saved. Let's connect with that promise. Make up your mind that nothing and no one can keep you from fulfilling God's will for your life and touching hearts for His kingdom, both believers' and seekers' hearts. Do this by adding touches of kindness and light (fruit of the Spirit (Galatians 5:22-23)), and offers of prayer or a listening ear, to people you know who need it, or to those God sends your way.

The Bible gives us an example of a king who wouldn't stay connected. He wanted to do his own thing. In 1 Kings 12, after King Solomon passed away, his son Rehoboam was made king. Solomon had built several magnificent buildings, and because of that, he'd had high taxes. When his son was made king, the people asked for some relief—lighter taxes and service.

Rehoboam told the people to give him three days to think about their request. He consulted his father's advisors, and they recommended that he work with the people and grant their request.

Rehoboam then consulted with his buddies. Here is how they answered.

"The young men who had grown up with him replied, 'Tell these people who have said to you, "Your father put a heavy yoke on us, but make our yoke lighter"—tell them, "My little finger is thicker than my father's waist. My father laid on you a heavy yoke; I will make it even heavier. My father scourged you with whips; I will scourge you with scorpions"'" (1 Kings 12:10-11).

That was bad advice. But Rehoboam immediately detached himself from wise counsel, liking the macho sound of his friends' advice. His response?

"The king answered the people harshly. Rejecting the advice given him by the elders, he followed the advice of the young men and said, 'My father made your yoke heavy; I will make it even heavier. My father scourged you with whips; I will scourge you with scorpions'" (1 Kings 12:13-14).

Unfortunately for Rehoboam, the scorpions were about to bite back.

"When all Israel saw that the king refused to listen to them, they answered the king:
>*'What share do we have in David,*
>*what part in Jesse's son?*
>*To your tents, O Israel!*
>*Look after your own house, O David!'*

So the Israelites went home. But as for the Israelites who were living in the towns of Judah, Rehoboam still ruled over them.

King Rehoboam sent out Adoniram, who was in charge of forced labor, but all Israel stoned him to death. King Rehoboam, however, managed to get into his chariot and escape to Jerusalem" (1 Kings 12:16-18).

The empire that had been magnificent under Kings David and Solomon now divided. Judah stayed with Rehoboam, but the rest of the kingdom made Jeroboam their king.

"So Israel has been in rebellion against the house of David to this day.

When all the Israelites heard that Jeroboam had returned, they sent and called him to the assembly and made him king over all Israel. Only the tribe of Judah remained loyal to the house of David" (1 Kings 12:19-20).

Everything began to unravel. Israel rebelled against the lineage of the house of David. War broke out. And Jeroboam feared he would lose his power if the people returned to Jerusalem to worship. So he built idols for the people to worship in Bethel and Dan (1 Kings 12:27-29).

King Jeroboam separated the people from their faith. He sold it as a convenience, but actually Jeroboam was more concerned about preserving his power base. The end result was that the people of God backslid (1 Kings 12:30). The nation spiritually exploded.

By NASA choosing the lunar orbit rendezvous system, the entire spacecraft was safer, and historic events took place.

Sooner or later, we come out ahead if we connect into what God is doing. He directs our every step. He knows the number of hairs on our head. He is a God of order and detail. Whatever we can do to subrogate our plans to God's purpose, will jumpstart our joy and illuminate our path.

The strongest connection. It is our connection with God's Word, ways, and will.

It was also a hatch that inexplicably sealed, following the prayers of a world that was connected to God. The hatch was "resurrected"—it functioned *again*.

Apollo 13, miracle number ten.

FAITH ACCELERATOR

Do you connect daily, or almost daily, with God's *Word*, the Bible? If not, pick a time you can spend time with Him in His Word each day, even if only for five or ten minutes. Quantity of time matters less than quality of time. Rather than just read, let the Bible speak to you, mentally placing yourself in each scene as it unfolds so that the Bible comes alive for you, as God intended.

Do you connect with Jesus' *ways* daily, showing kindness to and doing kindnesses for others? This not only lets His light shine in the world, it also fulfills the one doing it. Note simple ways you can show even more kindness to others. Add to your notes and reread these notes at least once each month.

Do you connect with God's *will* daily? His will is for each of us to touch seekers' hearts for His kingdom. Add your touches of kindness and light, and offers of prayer or a listening ear, to all who need it.

A firm connection leads to an inspired journey.

Apollo 13's damaged service module. Credit: NASA.

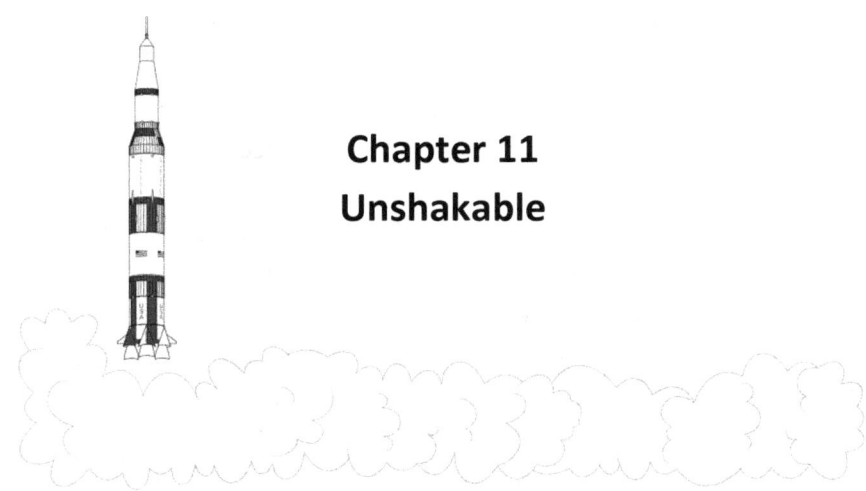

Chapter 11
Unshakable

Apollo 13 Miracle #11: The Command Module Wasn't Severed

April 17, 1970, GET 138:01 (Ground Elapsed Time 138 hours and 1 minute after liftoff)

As the command module floated near the edge of Earth's atmosphere, the crew jettisoned the service module to prepare for reentry. With camera in hand, they photographed as they observed for the first time the missing thirteen-foot high panel and the extent of the explosion damage.

Below the missing panel, at the bottom of the module, what appeared to be a shrapnel strike had caused a slight deformation of the bell-shaped service propulsion engine nozzle. Had that engine been fired . . .

"If the nozzle was deformed, surely there would have been a potentially fatal consequence of its firing, akin to the loss of the *Challenger* resulting from the failed solid rocket (SRB) engine," explained Jerry Woodfill.

Gene Kranz's gut feeling had been right.

What was more, the extent of damage revealed just how forceful an explosion it had been.

"The command module and service module remained connected following the explosion, while the internal pressure of the explosion rocketed the exterior panel into space," said Woodfill. "The attachment strength of the service module panel to the structure required a considerable internal pressure of 24 pounds per square inch for severing it from the service module. A much lower pressure was required to separate the command module with its heat shield from the service module, only 10 pounds per square inch. One can only speculate on why the panel blew and the crew capsule/service module attachment remained intact."

The Apollo 13 Failure Report revealed that the internal CM thermal problems may have become a serious threat had the CM been severed from the insulating service module. Instead of the spacecraft's internal temperature dropping to a near-freezing 34 degrees as it did, the astronauts could have experienced the influence of space temperatures nearing -134 degrees Fahrenheit.

The fact that the CM had not been blasted apart from the SM is yet another incident in the Apollo 13 mission that cannot be explained. But it preserved the lives of the three astronauts on board.

God's Firm Grip

It is imperative that we stay connected to our sources of strength when we deal with an explosion in our lives. The first thing the enemy wants to do is separate you and isolate you from what you need most. Staying connected to God, a good church, and the right people are necessary to survive an unexpected crisis in your life.

The Bible reveals that Satan goes about *"like a roaring lion looking for someone to devour" (1 Peter 5:8b)*. I've seen lions in the Serengeti and the savannahs of Africa patiently watching a herd of wildebeest. The lion is cleverly hidden. It waits for its opportunity. A young or wounded wildebeest who gets separated from the pack is quickly pounced upon by the predator.

Keep a firm grip on God, and He will keep a firm grip on you.

*"'So do not fear, for I am with you;
do not be dismayed, for I am your God.
I will strengthen you and help you;
I will uphold you with My righteous right hand'" (Isaiah 41:10).*

No hand is stronger, and no power is greater, than God's. In the end, the lion—the enemy—will lose.

"For I am convinced that neither death nor life, neither angels nor demons, neither the present nor the future, nor any powers, neither height nor depth, nor anything else in all creation, will be able to separate us from the love of God that is in Christ Jesus our Lord" (Romans 8:38-39).

It's Liberating to Be Limited

Soon after the explosion aboard Apollo 13, many people at Mission Control (the key word being "control") wanted the astronauts to fire the service module engine in an attempt to get them home fast. The idea that they would have to wait for the moon's gravity to turn the spacecraft around seemed like an insufferable limitation. They would be putting nature in the driver's seat.

Likewise some people hear the words "Ten Commandments" and think, "Ugh! Limitations!" It might not occur to them that it's liberating to be limited.

In 2 Corinthians, Paul shared his insights on this matter.

"Now if the ministry that brought death, which was engraved in letters on stone, came with glory, so that the Israelites could not look steadily at the face of Moses because of its glory, fading though it was, will not the ministry of the Spirit be even more glorious? If the ministry that condemns men is glorious, how much more glorious is the ministry that brings righteousness!" (2 Corinthians 3:7-9).

Paul called the gospel "the ministry of the Spirit," and described it as glorious. A few verses later, he added a second description.

"Now the Lord is the Spirit, and where the Spirit of the Lord is, there is freedom" (2 Corinthians 3:17).

Freedom. Some people at Mission Control thought going home the long way was limiting. Gene Kranz believed it would be freedom—liberty—for the astronauts. Like Paul, he saw that it can be *liberating* to be limited.

> **NASA Trivia:** Who made the following comment regarding Mars: "It's a fixer-upper of a planet but we could make it work"?[12]
>
> *(See footnote for answer.)*

What exactly is liberty? Because whatever liberty is, that is also what the Spirit of God embodies.

In our minds, we have an understanding of liberty as being something akin to the manifest expression of our wills. Liberty is freedom but freedom is not free. It must be valuable because men shed their blood to ensure its place in our nation's history. But

---

[12] Elon Musk, CEO of SpaceX, made the forward-looking comment in May 2013.

beyond that is spiritual freedom, which required Jesus' blood to be shed on Calvary.

To have liberty is to have an unfettered soul. It is oxygen to our souls. It is what makes our nature thrive and our spirits soar.

It comes from staying connected to God.

Patrick Henry, speaking on March 23, 1775 at St. John's Church in Richmond, Virginia, is credited with having swung the balance in convincing the Virginia House of Burgesses to pass a resolution to deliver Virginia troops to the Revolutionary War.

"They tell us, sir, that we are weak, unable to cope with so formidable an adversary. But when shall we be stronger? Will it be the next week, or the next year? Will it be when we are totally disarmed, and when a British guard shall be stationed in every house? Shall we gather strength by irresolution and inaction? Shall we acquire the means of effectual resistance by lying supinely on our backs and hugging the delusive phantom of hope, until our enemies shall have bound us hand and foot? Sir, we are not weak if we make a proper use of those means which the God of nature hath placed in our power. The millions of people, armed in the holy cause of liberty, and in such a country as that which we possess, are invincible by any force which our enemy can send against us. Besides, sir, we shall not fight our battles alone. There is a just God who presides over the destinies of nations, and who will raise up friends to fight our battles for us. The battle, sir, is not to the strong alone; it is to the vigilant, the active, the brave. Besides, sir, we have no election. If we were base enough to desire it, it is now too late to retire from the contest. There is no retreat but in submission and slavery! Our chains are forged! Their clanking may be heard on the plains of Boston! The war is inevitable—and let it come! I repeat it, sir, let it come.

"It is in vain, sir, to extenuate the matter. Gentlemen may cry, 'Peace, peace'—but there is no peace. The war is actually begun! The next gale that sweeps from the north will bring to our ears the clash of resounding arms! Our brethren are already in the field! Why stand we here idle? What is it that gentlemen wish? What would they have? Is life so dear, or peace so sweet, as to be purchased at the price of chains and slavery? Forbid it, Almighty God! I know not what course others may take; but as for me, give me liberty or give me death!"

Paul breaks down the liberty that faith gives in 2 Corinthians as well as any place in Scripture. He begins by stating that it is written in our hearts and it is read by all men.

"You show that you are a letter from Christ, the result of our ministry, written not with ink but with the Spirit of the living God, not on tablets of stone but on tablets of human hearts.

Such confidence as this is ours through Christ before God. Not that we are competent in ourselves to claim anything for ourselves, but our competence comes from God" (2 Corinthians 3:3-5).

We may sometimes see ourselves as being limited by God's will, but by staying within His will we are liberated in the Spirit.

By the command module not being severed, it wasn't limited. It was saved. The astronauts, photographing the wreckage, likely realized that it's liberating to be limited. Because of the "limitation," the CM hadn't been severed. It had been unshakable.

Limitations of Our Nature

True liberty begins with understanding our limitations as humans. That is why when we study the early history of the United States, God was a significant part of our decisions and our foundations as a nation. We recognized our limitations.

In a letter to his wife, Abigail, John Adams wrote that he thought our nation's birthday should be celebrated on the Fourth of July. He mentioned celebrations that would illuminate the sky, sounds that would proclaim the thunder of liberty, and in the same sentence he said, "a solemn expression of gratitude and devotion to our God." We got the fireworks down pat, but we seem to have lost the devotion to our God as part of a national expression of gratitude.

The Spirit of God is powerful beyond its eternal nature. It's powerful because of the perspective that it gives you. It puts everything in the right order. It gives you understanding that there is only one God, and it is not you. It is not me. And it is not our flesh, as much as our flesh would like to claim that role.

That understanding is liberating! I don't worry as much, because I know that God has it all under control and I am not expected to be God. I am not all knowing. I am not omnipresent. I am God's child, and it is liberating to know that I am not supposed to understand everything.

I used to think real freedom was getting a driver's license. Now I know real freedom is *not* having to drive. I used to be free from stress. I used to just ride in the back, look out the window, and let my dad take us from point A to point B.

It was liberating to be limited.

It's also liberating to know someone else is watching. I can sleep at night, knowing Someone Else is watching over me. I can laugh in hardship, because I know the One who controls the manna in heaven.

"He has made us competent as ministers of a new covenant—not of the letter but of the Spirit; for the letter kills, but the Spirit gives life" (2 Corinthians 3:6).

Limitations also enable us to live life free from despair. Jesus even said, *"'I am come that they might have life, and that they might have it more abundantly'" (John 10:10b KJV).*

Even the Constitution declared that there are inalienable rights that were given to man that guarantee life, liberty, and the pursuit of happiness.

An argument could be made that you are not really living as long as you are in bondage. If you're being controlled by the temptations of your flesh and the influence of unclean spirits, is that really living, or is it just existing?

144 | Chapter 11

What is real living? It's a life without shackles. It's a life free from the heaviness of guilt. How many people do you know who are in slavery? Slaves to alcohol. Slaves to drugs. Slaves to nicotine. Slaves to pornography. Slaves to idolatry, Slaves to lust. Slaves to sin.

Paul explained that the liberty we experience is bound up in the hope that we have in the glory of our God.

"Now if the ministry that brought death, which was engraved in letters on stone, came with glory, so that the Israelites could not look steadily at the face of Moses because of its glory, fading though it was, will not the ministry of the Spirit be even more glorious? If the ministry that condemns men is glorious, how much more glorious is the ministry that brings righteousness! For what was glorious has no glory now in comparison with the surpassing glory. And if what was fading away came with glory, how much greater is the glory of that which lasts!

Therefore, since we have such a hope, we are very bold" (2 Corinthians 3:7-12).

We, too, boldly trust in God's "limitations," because within them is liberty. In actuality, liberty is the opposite of death. Because true liberty is life.

Liberty is what the Spirit of God will do for you. That is what living in God will do. The limitations of our nature enable God to give us liberty.

Patrick Henry knew this. Gene Kranz knew this. Kranz's willingness to be limited in his control enabled God to keep the command module from being blown apart from the service module. Both men had trusted God's firm, unshakeable grip.

In the command module *Odyssey*, the astronauts took detailed photographs of the damaged service module. They had been saved again, because man had found liberty in his natural limitations and had trusted God to be in control. As a result, the laws of physics had gone out the window and had left their reentry capsule intact—safely within God's firm grip.

Apollo 13, miracle number eleven.

FAITH ACCELERATOR

Pen for yourself some reminders of challenging times you faced when God kept a tight hold on you and pulled you through.

Next, pen for yourself some reminders of challenging times you faced when God's limitations turned out to be liberating.

In future times of trouble, review your reminders. Be aware of the roaring lion, but hold on to the Lord who saves and gives liberty.

_____
_____
_____
_____
_____
_____
_____
_____
_____
_____
_____
_____
_____
_____
_____
_____
_____
_____
_____
_____

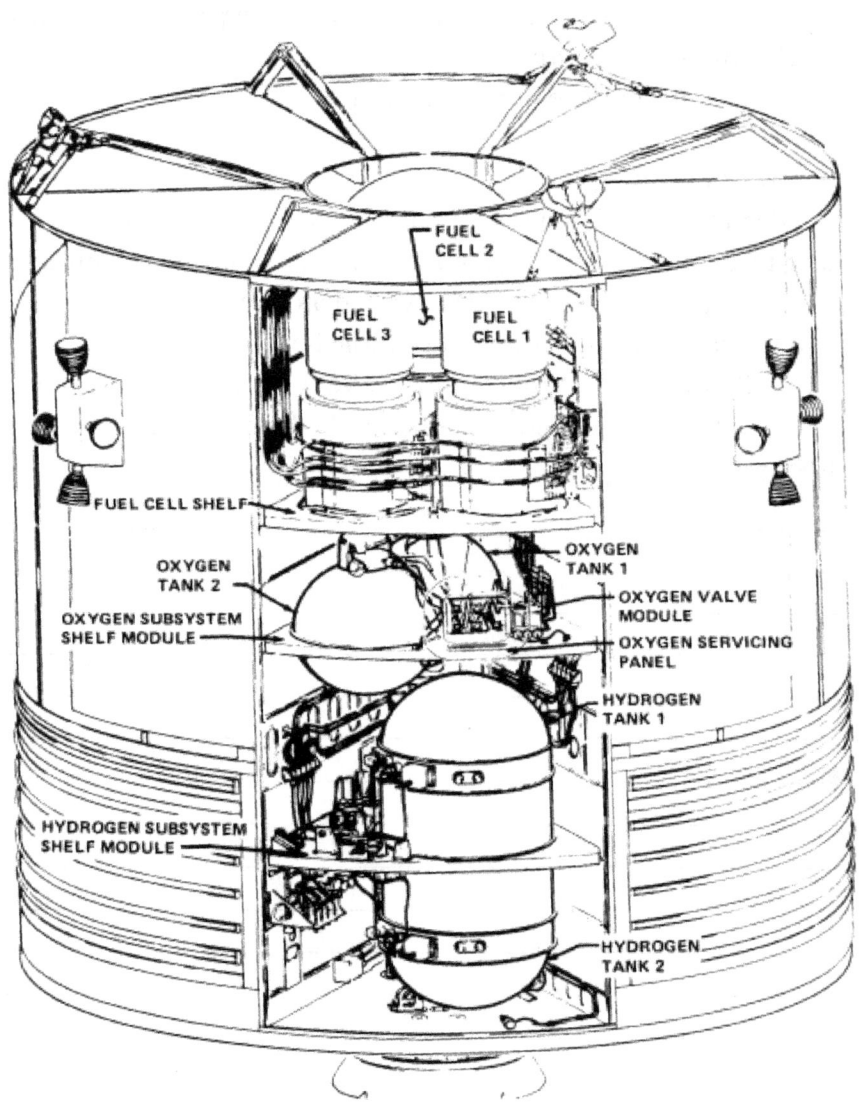

*Cutaway of the fuel cells and cryogenic tanks
in the Apollo 13 service module.
Credit: NASA.*

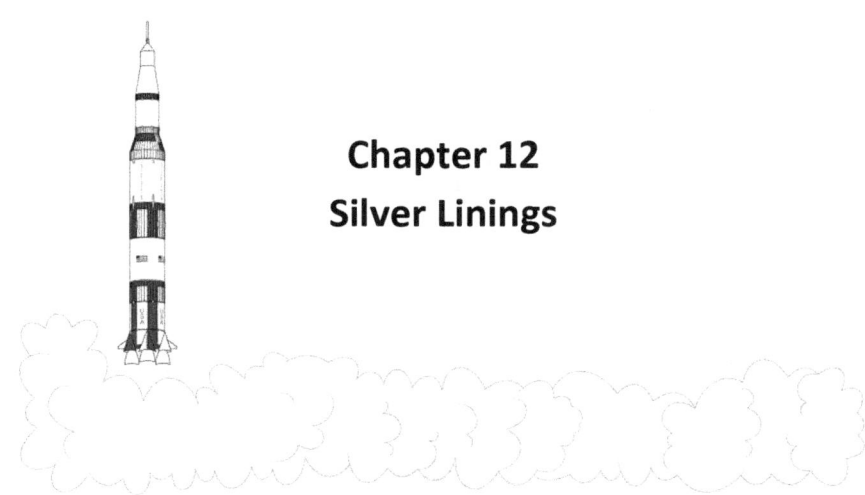

Chapter 12
Silver Linings

Apollo 13 Miracle #12: Placement of Oxygen Tank Two

As the astronauts continued photographing the damaged service module, they finally saw that the explosion had come from the area of the highly explosive oxygen tanks.

There were two oxygen tanks aboard the Apollo 13 spacecraft. Long before liftoff, the electrical wires of oxygen tank two's power fans were unknowingly damaged during a test, their insulation compromised.

NASA engineer Jerry Woodfill explained, "Because the spark which ignited the oxygen in tank two was located at the top of the tank, the tank acted like a cork on a Thermos bottle. Since it was [placed] on the outside perimeter [of the service module], it . . . blew out into space along with the thirteen-foot panel covering the side of the service module.

"The oxygen tank shelf served to isolate the explosion from the hydrogen tanks below. But had the inboard oxygen tank one exploded, likely this would not have been the case. Should the flawed tank have been the inner tank, its explosive force would have taken with it the sister O2 tank, amplifying the force of the explosion, just as using two sticks of dynamite instead of one; the destruction would be a magnitude greater.

"The added explosive force would have fractured the O2 tank shelf, involving the fragile hydrogen tanks below. The volatile hydrogen gas now having a wealth of oxygen from the overhead tanks would surely have destroyed the entire spacecraft assemblage. Of course, the crew would have immediately perished as well. There would have been no clues, no telemetry data trace to explain what had happened."

Woodfill added, "Oxygen tank one was given the inboard location adjacent to the flawed tank. Consider the likelihood of that placement."

He concluded, "I contend that the crew would have died if the flawed O2 tank two had not been on the outer perimeter of the service module. The position of that tank had much to do with the extent of the explosion's damage. Had tank one been damaged, no rescue would have been possible."

Their thoughts in awe and their photographing complete, the Apollo 13 crew stowed the camera and prepared to power up the command module. They were still unaware of the precise cause of the explosion, yet likely very thankful to be alive.

Tragedy-Inspired Appreciation

The way to maintain the proper perspective during revival of faith and recovery from difficult life events, is to always keep a thankful spirit. The challenge for our generation is that we have seen a decline in appreciation. It was prophesied in the Bible that, in end times, many people would become unthankful, even Christians.

"For although they knew God, they neither glorified Him as God nor gave thanks to Him, but their thinking became futile and their foolish hearts were darkened" (Romans 1:21).

An effective way to maintain a spirit of gratitude is to find a way to give thanks to those who are part of our team. The astronauts were deeply grateful for the tireless work of every person at Mission Control, and for the prayers of people around the world.

A spirit of thankfulness will build a team, and a spirit of unthankfulness will break down a team. It's hard to be a team player and be unthankful. They just go together.

I will only be used by God if I realize where my blessings come from. And I will only be thankful if I'm willing to admit that I need a team to help me stay on the path to heaven.

Here are three ways to keep a thankful spirit.

1. Worship God because He is God.

"I thank my God every time I remember you. In all my prayers for all of you, I always pray with joy because of your partnership in the gospel from the first day until now . . ." (Philippians 1:3-5).

2. Recognize that the spiritual people in your life are a gift from God.

Not only do we feel blessed when we express appreciation to others, but we also experience less stress when we know the weight of any given matter is not on us alone. Nor is a friend's burden on him or her alone; they have us to help them. Develop and grow good friendships with fellow believers, and then both will be blessed.

"A friend loves at all times,
and a brother is born for adversity" (Proverbs 17:17).

3. Find the good in every circumstance.

"Be joyful always; pray continually; give thanks in all circumstances, for this is God's will for you in Christ Jesus.
Do not put out the Spirit's fire . . ." (1 Thessalonians 5:16-19).

Living a life of thankfulness is the most enjoyable existence you can have. Though it will be difficult, look for the good in every circumstance, even when unexpected and difficult storms come at you.

The astronauts saw the extent of the damage, but they were thankful to be alive. Their tragedy-inspired appreciation enabled them to see the silver lining.

God's Strategic Plan and Placement

Life is messy. Plans go awry. Sometimes this is because we're embarking on a path we've decided is the right way to go, but then we find our forward momentum grinding to a halt. We don't understand it; we just know we are stuck. During the times God doesn't allow us to accomplish what we want, He has other plans for us. Sometimes the plans aren't obvious to us.

> *"In his heart a man plans his course,*
> *but the Lord determines his steps" (Proverbs 16:9).*

In many human endeavors, failure is the result of man becoming too self-sufficient or prideful about the accomplishment. God is more concerned about people than He is programs and plans. I've always been amazed at how much God loves people, even though it is humanity that oftentimes is the harshest critic of their Creator. This rejection by man does not equate to a loss of God's love for humanity. If we can just settle the issue that God loves mankind, we will be blessed.

And we will always be in the will of God if we love people as He does. As David told King Saul, *"'As surely as I valued your life today, so may the Lord value my life and deliver me from all trouble'" (1 Samuel 26:24).*

Following is the beginning of the story of David sparing Saul's life—a personal test for David, as you will see.

"The Ziphites went to Saul at Gibeah and said, 'Is not David hiding on the hill of Hakilah, which faces Jeshimon?'

So Saul went down to the Desert of Ziph, with his three thousand chosen men of Israel, to search there for David. Saul made his camp beside the road on the hill of Hakilah facing Jeshimon, but David stayed in the desert. When he saw that Saul had followed him there, he sent out scouts and learned that Saul had definitely arrived.

Then David set out and went to the place where Saul had camped. He saw where Saul and Abner son of Ner, the commander of the army, had lain down. Saul was lying inside the camp, with the army encamped around him.

David then asked Ahimelech the Hittite and Abishai son of Zeruiah, Joab's brother, 'Who will go down into the camp with me to Saul?'

'I'll go with you,' said Abishai.

So David and Abishai went to the army by night, and there was Saul, lying asleep inside the camp with his spear stuck in the ground near his head. Abner and the soldiers were lying around him.

Abishai said to David, 'Today God has delivered your enemy into your hands. Now let me pin him to the ground with one thrust of my spear; I won't strike him twice.'

But David said to Abishai, 'Don't destroy him! Who can lay a hand on the Lord's anointed and be guiltless? As surely as the Lord lives,' he said, 'the Lord Himself will strike him; either his time will come and he will die, or he will go into battle and perish. But the Lord forbid that I should lay a hand on the Lord's anointed. Now get the spear and water jug that are near his head, and let's go'" (1 Samuel 26:1-11).

From David's struggle in the above passage, and his understanding of God's strategic plan for him—including God's *strategic placement* of him, we can learn six insights.

1. God is concerned with more than just our victory. It is our nature to be focused on the finish line. Sometimes we're tempted to take the bait of "the end justifies the means." God never works like that. He's more concerned with the process.

David didn't always make the right decisions, but he was wise in this matter with Saul. He knew that God had placed Saul in God's hand, not David's. David realized that this placement was a chance for Saul to repent.

A person with less spiritual awareness would have seen Saul's sleeping as a favor from God and killed Saul on the spot, to secure the victory. Or killed Saul and justified it as the Lord putting Saul into David's hands, to secure the victory. But then David would have moved outside of God's strategic placement.

David also saw this for what it was: a test. For David, this was probably a tougher battle than Goliath. At least with Goliath, David had been able to recognize him as the enemy, but this test was different. A test that is hidden is harder to win.

In addition, David saw significance in the choice he made. Essentially he told Saul, "As I have been merciful to you, may God be merciful to me." David understood his and Saul's strategic placement in God's plan. Even when events and circumstances didn't make sense, he trusted his placement in God's will.

No doubt there are times in our walk with God that we question how we got where we are. We find ourselves saying, "If God is directing my path, then it's an unusual path that He has me on."

I can only imagine the number of times David questioned whether God was still on his side. David must have thought that God had lost his zip code. He'd been anointed king by the prophet Samuel, but the present king, Saul, chased David and tried to kill him. This chase was not over in a few days. King Saul was relentless in chasing David, for a number of years.

The Scriptures illustrate David's frustration. Paraphrased, "Why are you chasing me, Saul? Is it God? Is it you? Is it others forcing the issue?" David undoubtedly tried to make sense of the position he was in. He was attempting to be honorable. He had more than one opportunity to take the life of King Saul, but refused to lay a finger on him because of his respect for the anointed of God and his trust in God's strategic plan and placement.

God was concerned with more than David's victory.

Saul was a ticking time bomb. On the outside, he looked like a powerful king, but on the inside he was fragmented. He was eaten up with envy and insecurity. God was in the process of moving Saul to the outside and moving David to the inside. God knew that Saul was going to explode, so he positioned him outside of the presence of God, outside of the will of God, so that when he exploded—or more accurately, imploded—the damage would not cripple the nation of Israel.

"'As surely as I valued your life today, so may the Lord value my life and deliver me from all trouble'" (1 Samuel 26:24).

These words of David to Saul reveal that David recognized the principle of God's love for humanity. It was this revelation that returned David to the heart of God.

David learned to trust God's will, for both Saul and himself, knowing that God has a plan; He is concerned with more than just the victory.

2. Don't mistake a quick fix as a long-term solution. If David had killed Saul, then he would have been king over a fragmented country. He would have had Saul's blood on his hands, and he would have set in motion a bloody end to his own life.

Most problems that took time to develop will take time to dissolve. Don't go after the bait of instant gratification. The shortcut will oftentimes short circuit God's plan for your life.

When I was a young man, someone told me, "If you pay now, you can play later, but if you play now, you will pay later." I've found that to be valuable advice. If you discipline yourself now, you will reap the reward your entire life, but if you insist on living for the moment, you will always struggle.

If we truly want the will of God for our lives, we must reject the immediate "solution" for long-term satisfaction. We must live by confidence in, and sometimes the slow process of, God's strategic plan.

The path to God's plan for our lives is often littered with inexplicable events, loss, adversaries, discouragement, setbacks, and the temptation of fast resolutions. Avoid the quick fix, like David did. Wait for God to reveal the long-term solution.

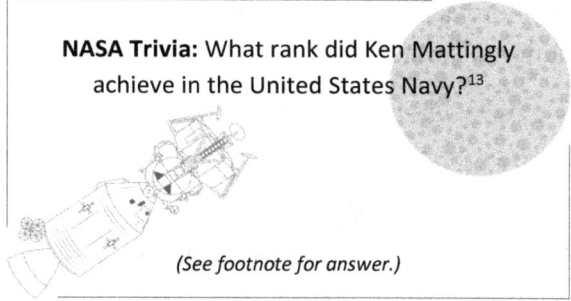

NASA Trivia: What rank did Ken Mattingly achieve in the United States Navy?[13]

(See footnote for answer.)

3. The process of moving you closer to the center of God's will is not always visible or obvious. God moves the pieces around on the chessboard in ways that we don't always see. We look at circumstances and events and see them as setbacks, but it could be that God is moving the pieces around to strategically place you in a position that He can use you in. What appears to be two steps back may be one step forward.

---

[13] Rear admiral. While he worked for NASA, he flew on the Apollo 16 mission, STS-4, and STS-51-C.

4. God may place you in a strategic position to win your adversary to the Lord. It seems counter-intuitive for us to think about the purpose of God in our adversaries' lives. We just assume that God is on our side, so our enemies must be His enemies. But God cares for each of us. He is working on both ends of the equation. God is the Savior of the world. That includes our nemeses.

He will give each of us a space of repentance, even our enemies.

It is during this time that we feel in spiritual limbo. This is when we have to trust God's plan for each stage of our lives. If we're following God's plan, we have to trust that He has us exactly where He wants us to be.

5. If someone you love spins out of God's will and away from faith, God will make provision for you to survive. There is no doubt that part of David's reasoning in not killing Saul when he had the chance was that David loved Saul and respected him as his king. This heart that David had is what drew the Lord to David to begin with.

David could not save Saul from Saul. Saul was on a path of destruction. David was wise to not be part of that spiritual suicide.

We would be wise to understand that God will protect those who live by Biblical principles. If you just hold on to the hand of God and trust Him, when the smoke clears, you will still be standing.

6. If there has been damage in the past, God will give place and opportunity for that hurt to be healed. If it is not fixed, it will be isolated. God will protect His church. The church is made up of people who are following God's will for their lives. He will reach for you and me, but if we reject help or we run down a destructive path, He will isolate the fallout so that the ship will survive.

Ultimately, our spiritual progress or demise is up to us. I am the only one who can defeat me, and you are the only one who can defeat you. This is why we must protect our thoughts and our eyes.

The road through life is not always paved with successes. Many times it is paved with setbacks, disappointments, and failures. But God's plans use the circumstances in our lives to bring about the right results.

I look at my own life and see where God has used apparent setbacks, disappointments, and failures to bring about reward, purpose, and fulfillment.

Success is the result of hard work, determination, and an utter trust in the providential hand of God. If we trust God through the storm, He will isolate the destruction of the storm, so that you and I will have a path of deliverance.

God's plan may have sparks and explosions, but it will get you safely home.

God saved astronauts Lovell, Swigert, and Haise from the explosion, though He stopped their mission to the moon. If God stops your forward momentum despite all your attempts to press on, know He has other plans for you. Look for an alternate path until you find it.

"'. . . Seek and you will find . . .'" (Matthew 7:7b).

The Blessing That Follows the Battle

I enjoyed reading *The Red Circle* by Brandon Webb. It's a book about a Navy SEAL sniper who served in Afghanistan and Iraq. He wrote about the training they went through, and how that training saved their lives more than once on the battlefield.

He trained some of the guys who took out Osama Bin Laden and the snipers who took out the Somalian pirates that had captured the American vessel off of Somalia.

These guys can hit a quarter at 1500 yards. They are the best in the world at what they do.

He wrote, "People always asked how the SEALs can do what they do. I have mentioned a number of times how fanatical about training we are in the SEALs. It's not really fanaticism though; it's realism. If you want to become not just competent, not just good, but outstanding, you have to train like a maniac at whatever it is you're intending to excel at—and then train some more."

He added, "I may have had a crazy childhood, wild and undisciplined in many ways, but one thing I'd always known was the rush that comes with pushing yourself hard, the thrill of seeing endless practice gradually producing a capacity for excellence. Beyond my own service in Afghanistan and the Gulf, my contribution to training a new generation of twenty-first century warriors would be based on this principle."

Blessing followed the battle.

Noted author and religious leader T.F. Tenney is quoted as saying, "God will not deliver you from something that He can develop you through." God may have some of us in boot camp right now. We're trying to make sense of the challenges we're going through. Could it be that he's trying to train spiritual warriors for the twenty-first century? If so, there is a tremendous blessing that is going to follow the battle.

That is what the astronauts discovered. That is what Paul discovered.

"If anyone else thinks he has reasons to put confidence in the flesh, I have more: circumcised on the eighth day, of the people of Israel, of the tribe of Benjamin, a Hebrew of Hebrews; in regard to the law, a Pharisee; as for zeal, persecuting the church; as for legalistic righteousness, faultless.

But whatever was to my profit I now consider loss for the sake of Christ. What is more, I consider everything a loss compared to the surpassing greatness of knowing Christ Jesus my Lord, for whose sake I have lost all things. I consider them rubbish, that I may gain Christ and be found in Him, not having a righteousness of my own that comes from the law, but that which is through faith in Christ—the righteousness that comes from God and is by faith. I want to know Christ and the power of His resurrection and the fellowship of sharing in His sufferings, becoming like Him in His death, and so, somehow, to attain to the resurrection from the dead.

Not that I have already obtained all this, or have already been made perfect, but I press on to take hold of that for which Christ Jesus took hold of me. Brothers, I do not consider myself yet to have taken hold of it. But one thing I do: Forgetting what is behind and straining toward what is ahead, I press on toward the goal to win the prize for which God has called me heavenward in Christ Jesus" (Philippians 3:4b-14).

Paul had a transformation where he had to dismiss his accomplishments and embrace his sufferings, for one reason—so he might obtain Christ. He was still a warrior, he had the heart of a warrior, but he had to be retrained for God's army.

God loves warriors. People are sometimes confused as to why David was a man after the heart of God. Why did God love David so much? David sinned. He slaughtered people. He made bad decisions. But the Lord looks at the heart. We think of David playing songs and tip-toeing through the tulips with a harp. No. David was a warrior. David was fearless.

God looks at the heart, and David was a warrior in his heart.

Peter was a warrior. Paul was a warrior. God loves warriors.

In Acts 16 we read that God's Word was gaining traction in Philippi. Some people started to come to God. Lydia was a businesswoman, and she was baptized with her household. After that a lady was delivered from an evil spirit, a spirit of divination.

Things were going well. God was moving. God was saving. God was delivering.

Then Paul and Silas were thrown into jail. Not just jail, but the inner prison, and then in stocks. Not just thrown in, but beaten and whipped and tossed into the slammer. They might have thought, "Hey, God, we're here doing your work. Why did this happen?"

God didn't tell them that this had happened so the jailer in the prison could be saved. It would've been nice to have known that up front, but God rarely tells us up front. However, when the apostles started singing, when they started worshipping, God indicated, "They've got this lesson. Move straight to jail break."

The jailer and his household were saved. In Philippi, things moved from a couple of people being saved to a revival that shook the whole city.

In Acts 19, Ephesus was a tough nut to crack. This was a wealthy city that was full of schools, libraries, and all kinds of witchcraft. God was good, and Paul found some disciples of John. Paul taught for about three months in the synagogue, and used his education to teach in the schools for two years. People started burning their witchcraft books and having revival, and then all of hell broke loose. The Bible describes it as "no small stir."

Paul had to flee to Macedonia for his life, but the revival flourished in Ephesus.

It wasn't the only time Paul fled for his life. But blessings followed the battles. Every time there was a setback, every time there was a battle, God came back with an even bigger blessing.

I can't even begin to tell you how many battles and setbacks I have had, but God always comes back with an even greater blessing.

God has something big for you. When you battle, know without any doubt that blessing will follow.

Aboard the Apollo 13 service module, oxygen tank two had exploded. Immediately after, at Mission Control, a battle had followed to save the crew. But God already had saved the men. He'd seen to it that the damaged oxygen tank had been placed at the outer perimeter of the service module, so the tragedy could inspire appreciation, and so a blessing could follow the battle. He'd provided silver linings.

Apollo 1 interior after the fire. Credit: NASA.

The Tragic Fire That Saved Apollo 13

Three and a half years prior to the launch of Apollo 13, Apollo 1 astronauts Gus Grissom, Ed White, and Roger Chaffee were tragically killed in a flash fire that erupted in the command module during a test at Kennedy Space Center. The pure oxygen atmosphere proved fatal before anyone, inside the module or out, could open the hatch.

As a result, NASA updated to a mixed-gas pad atmosphere of nitrogen combined with oxygen for future Apollo spacecraft. In addition, they coated all command module electrical connections and switch contacts to render them moisture proof and fireproof.

One thinks of the horrific sacrifice of Grissom, White, and Chaffee and can't help but honor them as three of the greatest heroes of America's space program, alongside those who did dare, and succeed, to travel into space. Because of these three men, the Apollo program continued, and advanced.

But more importantly, the moisture coating and fireproofing of electrical connections that were implemented as a result of the Apollo 1 fire now enabled Lovell, Swigert, and Haise to power up their frosty command module in preparation for reentry . . . and survive.

If the Apollo 1 tragedy has a silver lining, it's that its crew's sacrifice enabled countless others who came after them to persevere.

The command module was able to power up because a "chance" oxygen tank placement had prevented the entire spacecraft from exploding days earlier, when O2 tank two had ignited.

This brought about tragedy-inspired appreciation, and sure knowledge that blessings follow the battles.

Apollo 13, miracle number twelve.

FAITH ACCELERATOR

Write twenty things you see around you right now that you are thankful for.

Next, list times God provided a blessing to follow a battle in your life.

Develop and maintain the habit of praising God for the good rather than complaining about the bad. For example, instead of grumbling about having to wash dishes or laundry, thank God for the food, plates, and clothes. Instead of criticizing a family member's quirks or ways they annoy you (whether criticizing aloud or silently), mentally list five things you like about them.

Worship God, be thankful for friends and family, find the good in every circumstance, know that God strategically places you, and trust God to send blessings after the battles. Then God, your friends and family, and your own spirit will be your buoys during the storms.

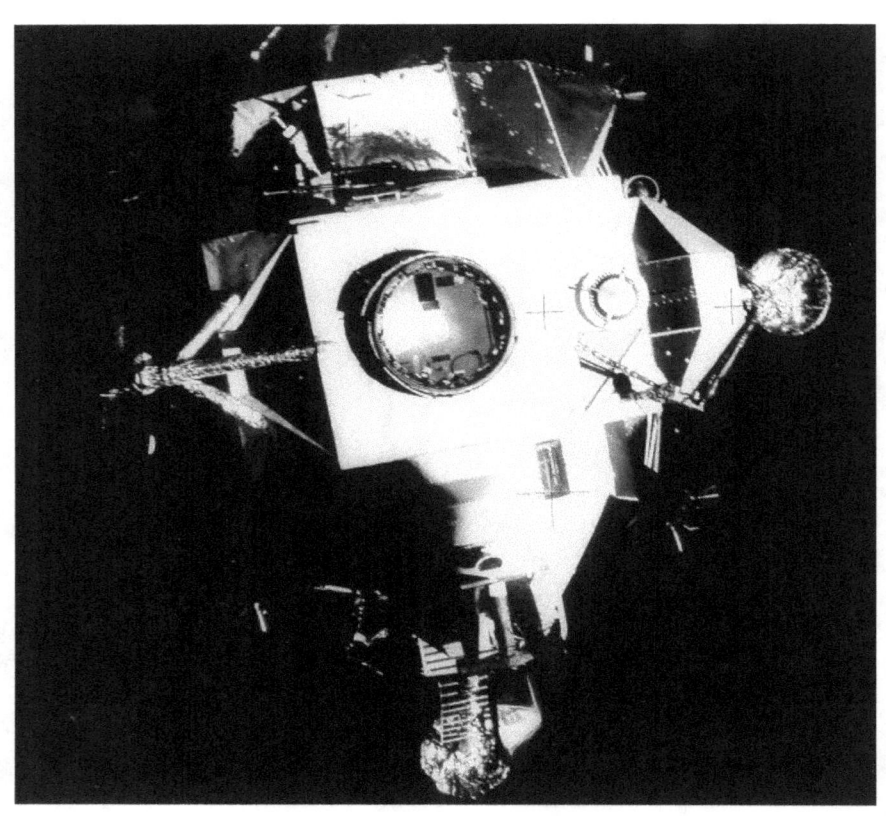

Top view of the lunar module Aquarius *after separation. April 17, 1970. Credit: NASA.*

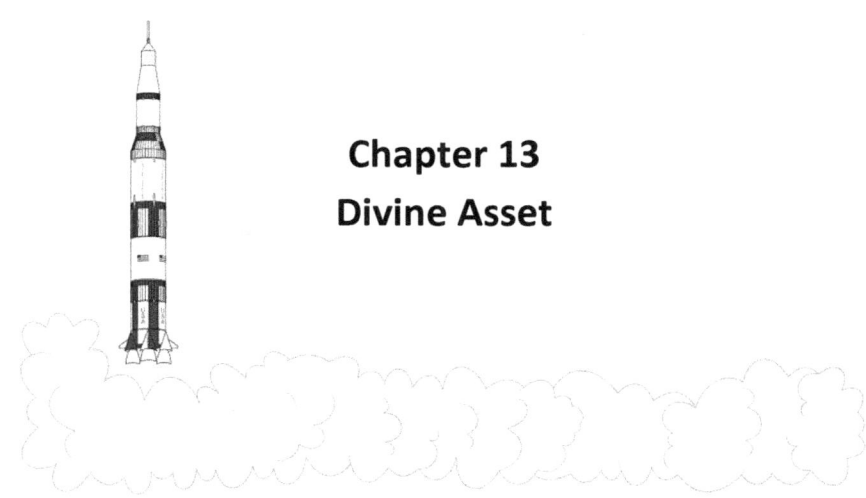

Chapter 13
Divine Asset

Apollo 13 Miracle #13: The Heat Shield
April 17, 1970, GET 141:30

The astronauts had jettisoned their lunar module lifeboat, the *Aquarius*, and the service module. As the two modules drifted away from the conical CM capsule, the *Odyssey*, the men strapped into their seats for reentry. A significant concern remained: the heat shield. The fact that the explosion hadn't severed the command module from the SM not only had kept the internal temperature from diving below 34 degrees, it also had protected the heat shield. Or so hoped the crew, Mission Control, and people around the world who prayed fervently and watched breathlessly the final events of the mission unfold live on the news.

And if the SM *hadn't* been able to protect the heat shield? "The fiery bazooka-like blast of the explosion might have cracked the heat shield and damaged critical parts of that engine," Woodfill revealed.

How would the world know if the heat shield had been damaged? Either the *Odyssey* would burn up during reentry through Earth's atmosphere, or it would splash down in the Pacific Ocean, intact.

At GET 142:40, the *Odyssey* left the edge of space and descended into Earth's atmosphere.

An extended blackout of communications followed. Then communications returned. Astronauts Jim Lovell, Jack Swigert, and Fred Haise splashed safely down in the Pacific Ocean aboard the *Odyssey*, still alive, and cold, due to the protective insulation of an undamaged heat shield.

A Spiritual Heat Shield

I believe that each of us has a heat shield in our spiritual life. This heat shield is protected when we stay connected to our spiritual covering. Our heat shield has to be protected for us to survive this life. The shield of faith and faithfulness protects us from hell and its fiery darts.

Staying connected to God, the Bible, and helpful Christian peers will not only save us from eternal judgment, but it will also help us deal with the heat of this world. The heat of adversity. The heat of criticism. The heat of false witnesses. The heat of rejection and loss.

Why did I specify "helpful" Christian peers? Have you ever noticed that when you're at a low point or you're dealing with an explosion of some sort in your life, it seems like others will pile on and only make things more difficult?

Elisha stayed with Elijah as long as he could because he knew there was heat coming from the fifty sons of the prophets who were waiting for him (2 Kings 2:7). These sons of the prophets were critics. They could do it better . . . or so they thought. They had already started telling Elisha that his master would be taken from him (2 Kings 2:3). This is the crowd that is always telling you how you are supposed to do your job. They had a position (sons of the prophets), so they thought they had authority.

Heat can sometimes come from someone or a group of people who think they've figured out what you're struggling with. They may even be well intentioned, but they're not helping. Their interference just causes the crisis you're dealing with to be more intense. If this is the case, politely shield yourself from them and connect with someone else. Perhaps someone who is more of a listener.

"Like one who takes away a garment on a cold day,
or like vinegar poured on soda,
is one who sings songs to a heavy heart" (Proverbs 25:20).

"My dear brothers, take note of this: Everyone should be quick to listen, slow to speak and slow to become angry . . ." (James 1:19).

Even the disciples made this blunder, probably without realizing it. They essentially asked Jesus, "Who has sinned, this man or his parents, that he was born blind?" (John 9:2). The man was blind, and that would be difficult enough, but now he had to deal with the disciples thinking that he was a sinner or that he had bad parents. The Lord fixed it by saying, "Neither."

That is the way God works. He is our divine asset. He safeguards our heat shield. If you stay attached to Him and His Word, your spirit is protected. Your attitude—your ability to endure—is protected. The biggest mistake people can make during a crisis is to jettison from the Command Module too soon, thinking that the principles of God's Word and the sacrifices of a disciplined lifestyle are just dead weight.

Elisha refused to be separated from his master too soon. Even when Elijah told him to "stay here," Elisha refused. He kept telling Elijah, "I will not leave you" (2 Kings 2:2).

Here is how the rest of the story plays out.

"As they were walking along and talking together, suddenly a chariot of fire and horses of fire appeared and separated the two of them, and Elijah went up to heaven in a whirlwind. Elisha saw

this and cried out, 'My father! My father! The chariots and horsemen of Israel!' And Elisha saw him no more. Then he took hold of his own clothes and tore them apart.

He picked up the cloak that had fallen from Elijah and went back and stood on the bank of the Jordan. Then he took the cloak that had fallen from him and struck the water with it. 'Where now is the Lord, the God of Elijah?' he asked. When he struck the water, it divided to the right and to the left, and he crossed over.

The company of the prophets from Jericho, who were watching, said, 'The spirit of Elijah is resting on Elisha.' And they went to meet him and bowed to the ground before him. 'Look,' they said, 'we your servants have fifty able men. Let them go and look for your master. Perhaps the Spirit of the Lord has picked him up and set him down on some mountain or in some valley.'

'No,' Elisha replied, 'do not send them'" (2 Kings 2:11-16).

Immediately, there was friction. This was Elisha having to reenter the real world. Just like the command module that had to reenter Earth's atmosphere, Elisha had to reenter this hostile environment. Elisha, up to this point, had enjoyed the comfort of Elijah's shadow. Not very much heat in the shadow. But now that his mentor had departed, he felt the heat of the crowd.

It seems clear that when we lose the connection of our faith in tumultuous times, we lose the stability that is needed at the most crucial times in our lives. We lose our spiritual heat shields. There is something about storms and explosions that strain our connection points, especially connections that are based in Biblical principles.

I remember a time a few years back when I reeled from an unexpected event. I was praying for God to help me to have clarity of judgment and protect my spirit. The Lord gave me just two words: "Stay connected." I knew I had to stay on the vine and stay connected to God. I made up my mind that I would stay with the Bible, even when it didn't seem to make sense in my situation.

"'I am the vine; you are the branches. If a man remains in Me and I in him, he will bear much fruit; apart from Me you can do nothing'" (John 15:5).

There is no connection stronger than the tenacity of a heat shield of faith in God. Uncracked, undamaged trust in Him enables us to withstand the heat of troubles and crises that we must move through in life. And God will never leave us.

"'I am with you always, to the very end of the age'" (Matthew 28:20b).

Our faith—our trust in God—is our heat shield in life. We might not always understand what He does, but we'll trust Him, come what may.

> *"'If you do not stand firm in your faith,*
> *you will not stand at all'" (Isaiah 7:9b).*

"Now faith is being sure of what we hope for and certain of what we do not see. This is what the ancients were commended for" (Hebrews 11:1-2).

"Abram believed the Lord, and He credited it to him as righteousness" (Genesis 15:6).

"'. . . Your faith has made you well'" (Luke 17:19b).

This spiritual heat shield also remains solid when we adopt self-discipline as His followers, and not halfhearted dedication as mere fans.

"Then He said to them all: 'If anyone would come after Me, he must deny himself and take up his cross daily and follow Me'" (Luke 9:23).

"'And anyone who does not carry his cross and follow Me cannot be My disciple'" (Luke 14:27).

It seems like saying no to one thing is the equivalent of saying yes to something else. If I say no to the flesh then I am saying yes to the Spirit (fasting is an example). If I say no to man's philosophy, I am saying yes to Biblical principles. If I want God's will, I may have to say no to man's will, or my own.

If we refuse to believe we'll incinerate amid Earth's atmosphere of unbelief, then we implicitly trust that God will bring us through it, and will bolster faith—ours and possibly that of others—as a result.

And, similar to Elijah and Elisha, our separation from our faith mentors and teachers will happen at the appointed time. It will happen with the hand of God. You don't have to force it. Just like the command module and the service module, the detachment will happen at the ordained time. Anything before that is risky.

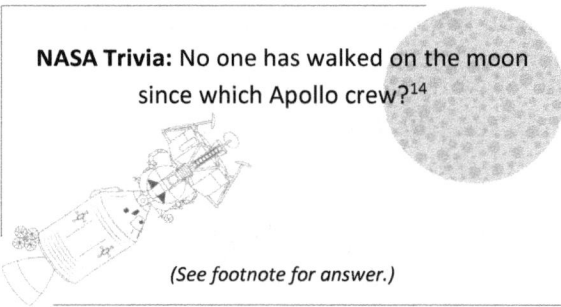

NASA Trivia: No one has walked on the moon since which Apollo crew?[14]

(See footnote for answer.)

When Explosions Strike

The astronauts weren't the only ones to have a divine Heat Shield. King David of the Old Testament relied greatly on God's protection, particularly when explosions struck.

---

[14] Apollo 17. Commander Gene Cernan stepped from the surface to the ladder of the LM on December 14, 1972—more than forty years ago.

Of all the battles that King David faced, perhaps none of them was more severe than the battle of Ziklag. David had left with his men to fight with the Philistines, who were protecting him and his army from King Saul. The Philistines could tell that David's heart wasn't in it. They sent David and his men home to Ziklag where they and their families had been camped.

When David and his men arrived, they found out that the Amalekites had invaded their camp, taken their families captive, and burned the camp. The men were already tired, and when this attack became obvious to them, they lifted up their voices and wept.

The men in their grief and heartache turned on David, their leader, and sought to kill him. David then prayed and asked God, David's divine Heat Shield, what to do. God directed him to pursue the Amalekites. David and his men did, and were able to recover their families and all of their possessions.

Only two days after David returned from chasing and subduing the Amalekites, news came: King Saul was dead. Saul had been chasing David and seeking to kill him for years. David and his men had been forced to live in caves and dwell in the wilderness, all because of Saul's jealousy and fear of David. Now Saul was dead.

Right before deliverance came to David, the last-minute battle with the Amalekites almost took him and his men out. Just moments before being made king, his and his men's entire families had been captured, and his men had determined to kill him.

Right before God blesses you with a miracle, there will first be a fire. A storm. A crisis. The key is to know how to deal with the fire when it comes.

How did David deal with it?

1. David encouraged himself in the Lord.

"David was greatly distressed because the men were talking of stoning him; each one was bitter in spirit because of his sons and

daughters. But David found strength in the Lord his God" (1 Samuel 30:6).

Sometimes you just have to encourage yourself. No one else will do it. You don't feel like it. Everything looks bleak, but you can encourage yourself in the Lord by remembering how he's helped you through trouble before.

2. David worshipped.

The ephod was a garment that the priest had worn ever since the tabernacle had been constructed in the wilderness. Likely styled similar to a chef's apron, Exodus 28 reveals the ephod was made of linen cloth with a myriad of colors around the waist. It had two onyx stones that were engraved with the twelve tribes of Israel, six names on each stone.

The priests would wear the ephod into the tabernacle. Wearing it signified that they were going into the presence of God. It was very specific to the priesthood and to people who were committed to the service of God. The ephod represented a time and place where humanity inquired of God. Where people were dependent on the move of the Holy Spirit.

When David said "bring me the Ephod" (1 Samuel 30:7), he signaled that he was going to worship. He was going to lean on the strength of God.

The Bible says the Lord will take your spirit of heaviness and replace it with a garment of praise (Isaiah 61:3). This life that we live has fiery trials, but God gives us an answer to the heaviness of disappointment. The solution is to praise. Find a way to worship God, and it will lift your spirits.

> *"I call to the Lord, who is worthy of praise,*
> *and I am saved from my enemies" (Psalm 18:3).*

3. David prayed.

"And David inquired of the Lord, 'Shall I pursue this raiding party? Will I overtake them?'

'Pursue them,' He answered. 'You will certainly overtake them and succeed in the rescue'" (1 Samuel 30:8).

If you get into a crisis, you will find a way to pray. You don't have to be coaxed or encouraged to pray. You will pray as a matter of necessity.

Prayer is powerful when it is based on a consistent life of prayer. God is responsive to emergency prayer, but prayer born in the fire of adversity will pay dividends for any situation in life.

4. David went.

"David and the six hundred men with him came to the Besor Ravine . . ." (1 Samuel 30:9a).

God honors action. Movement. Just go to the service. Just go to the altar. Just go to the prayer meeting. You might not have it all figured out yet, but go. Move toward your answer. God will provide it.

During the Apollo 1 fire, a man who attended our church in Palm Bay was sitting in the bunker near the launch pad monitoring the test from his screens. When he saw the fire ignite within the command module, he screamed. The safety officer next to him froze.

Our man jumped over him, grabbed the fire extinguisher, and rushed to the launch gantry. But it was too late.

Sometimes you have a window of opportunity, and you have to do something or the moment will pass.

5. David pursued.

". . . Two hundred men were too exhausted to cross the ravine. But David and four hundred men continued the pursuit" (1 Samuel 30:10).

This is commitment. David not only went, he pursued. This is stronger. This is chasing. This is being focused on a goal and going after it. This wasn't easy for David and the four hundred men, considering the emotional state they were in and that a third of their army didn't join them.

Two hundred men were so heart-stricken that they couldn't go any further. These were courageous men, warriors. They were not people who called in sick. They weren't afraid of a fight. But their discouragement was so pronounced, they couldn't even join the posse and pursue the enemy.

Sometime we can be so overtaken with grief or sorrow that we can't even do what our natural instinct is to do. Something just shuts down. This is when we have to make decisions based on the Word of God and not our emotions. Our emotions can fool us and give us false information. Pursue.

6. David said.

"They found an Egyptian in a field and brought him to David. They gave him water to drink and food to eat—part of a cake of pressed figs and two cakes of raisins. He ate and was revived, for he had not eaten any food or drunk any water for three days and three nights.

David asked him, 'To whom do you belong, and where do you come from?'

He said, 'I am an Egyptian, the slave of an Amalekite. My master abandoned me when I became ill three days ago. We raided the Negev of the Kerethites and the territory belonging to Judah and the Negev of Caleb. And we burned Ziklag.'

David asked him, 'Can you lead me down to this raiding party?'

He answered, 'Swear to me before God that you will not kill me or hand me over to my master, and I will take you down to them'" (1 Samuel 30:11-15).

Silence is not golden when you are in chaos. You have to open your mouth and speak. Don't isolate yourself. The enemy likes to pounce on a wounded spirit and try to convince you to remove yourself from your spiritual support. Don't take the bait. Stay connected and talk it out with people you can trust.

David didn't kill the Egyptian they had found. When you are in trouble, you have to be able to discern the difference between friend and foe. Don't automatically reject people whom God may have put in your path to help you. Speak. Inquire. You have to know when to use your sword, and you have to know when to use your mouth.

Speak. There is power in the tongue. Declare the promises of God, your divine asset.

7. David struck.

"He led David down, and there they were, scattered over the countryside, eating, drinking and reveling because of the great amount of plunder they had taken from the land of the Philistines and from Judah.

David fought them from dusk until the evening of the next day, and none of them got away, except four hundred young men who rode off on camels and fled" (1 Samuel 30:16-17).

You have to destroy what is trying to destroy you. You have to strike down the enemy. Don't let sin coopt your mind and coexist in your home. Kill off that thought. Kill off that feeling. Don't try to manage it. Don't let it live.

Take authority over it. Take the victory. God has given you the victory. Take it.

It frustrates me when people will not fight for themselves or for their families when explosions hit. FIGHT. God will fight for you, but you have to fight for yourself. Fight for your soul. Stay at the plate and keep swinging. Eventually you will hit the ball. You will hit it out of the park.

8. David recovered.

"David recovered everything the Amalekites had taken, including his two wives. Nothing was missing: young or old, boy or girl, plunder or anything else they had taken. David brought everything back. He took all the flocks and herds, and his men drove them ahead of the other livestock, saying, 'This is David's plunder'" (1 Samuel 30:18-20).

It may not seem like it right now, but God will return everything that the enemy has taken from you. It may be a family member or a friend. It may be a job or a house. It may be your physical or emotional health. Regardless of what it is, you can get it all back.

He is the master of the return. Not only is Jesus going to return to this Earth one day, He is going to return us to glory. God created us and is going to come back for us. He is going to return principalities and powers to their place of judgment. Everything will return at the voice of God. In the meantime, don't you think He has the power to return your stuff to you?

9. David showed mercy.

"Then David came to the two hundred men who had been too exhausted to follow him and who were left behind at the Besor Ravine. They came out to meet David and the people with him. As David and his men approached, he greeted them. But all the evil men and troublemakers among David's followers said, 'Because

they did not go out with us, we will not share with them the plunder we recovered. However, each man may take his wife and children and go.'

David replied, 'No, my brothers, you must not do that with what the Lord has given us. He has protected us and handed over to us the forces that came against us. Who will listen to what you say? The share of the man who stayed with the supplies is to be the same as that of him who went down to the battle. All will share alike.' David made this a statute and ordinance for Israel from that day to this" (1 Samuel 30:21-25).

The Bible makes it clear that God is merciful to us in proportion to how merciful we are to others. Forgiveness sets us free and releases healing properties in our spirits.

Release the feelings that are holding you hostage spiritually. Bitterness is a spiritual cancer. Release the hurt. This can only happen by showing mercy to someone you don't have to, but you choose to. It is liberating.

10. David was generous.

"When David arrived in Ziklag, he sent some of the plunder to the elders of Judah, who were his friends, saying, 'Here is a present for you from the plunder of the Lord's enemies.'

He sent it to those who were in Bethel, Ramoth Negev and Jattir; to those in Aroer, Siphmoth, Eshtemoa and Racal; to those in the towns of the Jerahmeelites and the Kenites; to those in Hormah, Bor Ashan, Athach and Hebron; and to those in all the other places where David and his men had roamed" (1 Samuel 30:26-31).

You have to share the blessing . . . or the blessing will be cut off.

The fire of adversity will produce a harvest, but you have to be able to handle it. You handle it by giving it away. You handle it by keeping your hand open. A professor at seminary told me that if you will keep an open hand, God will continue to fill it.

The Apollo program was almost cancelled before man ever got to the moon. The fire had to be endured before the mission could be accomplished. The fire took its toll, and the ultimate sacrifice was paid by the families of the Apollo 1 astronauts.

I started in the ministry working with young people. I've seen young people face the fire of adversity early in life. It seems that the young people who have the most potential face the greatest challenges. The fire produces strength and anointing if it is endured, but make no mistake, there will be fire. There will be a test.

It is how God purifies silver and gold.

> "For You, O God, tested us;
> You refined us like silver.
> . . . But You brought us to a place of abundance"
> (Psalm 66:10, 12c).

> "But He knows the way that I take;
> when He has tested me, I will come forth as gold" (Job 23:10).

God purifies us, and while doing so He helps us through it, protecting us. He is our divine asset. Our spiritual Heat Shield.

After more than a dozen malfunctions and crises that repeatedly threatened their lives, astronauts Jim Lovell, Jack Swigert, and Fred Haise bobbed on top the Pacific Ocean in the capsule *Odyssey*, awaiting retrieval by the Navy. Their endangered mission had come to an end. The men had survived reentry, because of the protective insulation of an undamaged heat shield.

Apollo 13, miracle number thirteen.

FAITH ACCELERATOR

Write the above 1 Samuel Bible references. When explosions strike in your life, look up the passages and remember David's example of dealing with troubles. God may test you so that He can bless you.

During your next personal Bible study, use your Bible's index of topics or a concordance to explore the topics of *faith* and *trust*. As you conduct your research, list your favorite faith and trust Bible verses in the lines provided so you can easily find the passages again. Review these passages that are most meaningful to you if ever you perceive a crack beginning to form in your spiritual heat shield. Then pray, and trust in God's love, presence, and plans.

Apollo 13 astronauts Fred Haise, Jack Swigert, and Jim Lovell, safe aboard the primary recovery ship, USS Iwo Jima. *April 17, 1970. Credit: NASA.*

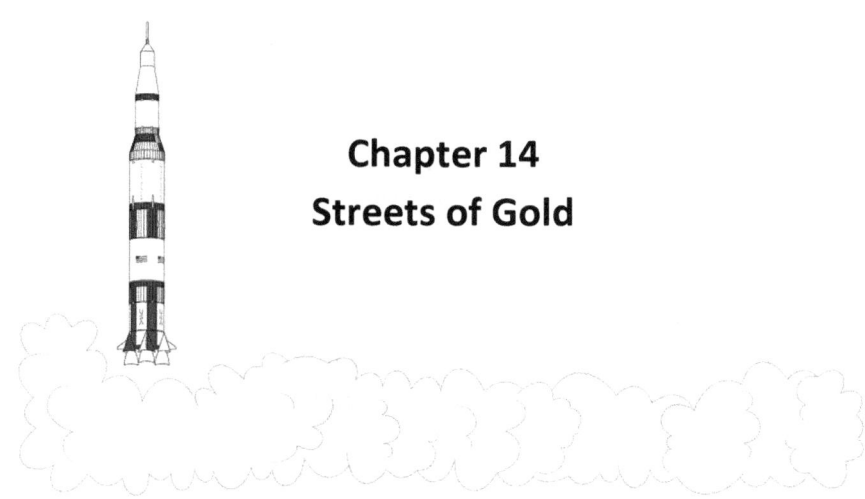

Chapter 14
Streets of Gold

A Successful Failure

Through a series of miraculous events and engineering marvels, the Apollo 13 astronauts survived an explosion on their spacecraft while in space and returned safely to Earth. The mission has come to be called a "successful failure."

Jerry Woodfill said, "The more I study these unexplainable events, the more convinced I am that God had His hand on these people and allowed a mistake to transform into a miracle right before our eyes."

Perhaps that's why God allowed the problems aboard Apollo 13 to occur, while enabling the astronauts to survive. He has revealed to all humanity that, though He typically provides miracles (both small and large) to individuals one on one, occasionally He still reminds the world as a whole that ultimately all power and love and salvation come through Him.

From Failure to Freedom

As imperfect humans, we often fail. Moses had some doozies.

Moses was raised in Pharaoh's palace as a son, but one day his passion for his people got the best of him. After seeing many

Egyptians beat their Hebrew captives, he finally couldn't take it anymore. He rose up and struck an Egyptian guard responsible for many beatings and killed him.

Quickly Moses buried the Egyptian in the sand, but others saw it and word got out. Pharaoh learned of it and tried to kill Moses (Exodus 2:15).

Moses ran for his life. He ended up in the wilderness, tending sheep for a living.

He must have replayed that murder scene over and over in his mind. The act that drove him from the palace. The act that drove him out of Egypt.

He must have thought his life was over. But God had a plan. God had seen to it that Moses had identified with the Hebrews, and not with the strong arm of the Egyptian army that he had grown up with. And the Hebrews, because two of them had seen the murder and told their friends about it, came to identify with Moses and view him as their defender.

That "failure" was a successful failure, because God made it so. God used it to free the Hebrew people.

Likewise, God can turn your failure into freedom. Freedom from sin.

There was a long gap in time during which Moses looked after sheep, but finally the Lord called Moses. It happened while Moses stood before a bush that was on fire but not consumed.

God told Moses, "Take off your shoes, because you're standing on holy ground." Then God asked Moses, "What's in your hand?"

"A staff," Moses replied.

Then God told Moses, "Throw down your staff."

Moses did, and the staff became a snake (Exodus 4).

When Moses threw his staff down, he was throwing down his identity . . . as a shepherd. He was throwing down his security. The staff had protected him and his flock against the numerous wilderness predators. It took a lot to throw down his staff, and when it became a snake . . .

I can just imagine Moses thinking, "I knew I should have held on to it! I end up throwing away everything that has any value, and I know this was the wrong thing to do, because now it's a snake and it's going to attack me!"

Sometimes when we obey God, it appears that we received the wrong result. We simply obeyed God, but then the bottom fell out. Remember that inside of every failure is the DNA of a miracle.

Next the Lord told Moses to pick up the snake.

WHAT?!

A snake? If you're like me, all snakes are evil. They are not to be handled; they are to be destroyed. Sooner rather than later. And now Moses was told to pick up the snake? I believe the Lord feels the same way I do, because He told Moses to pick up the serpent by the tail (Exodus 4:4).

Moses obeyed (after all, a bush is talking to him). He picked up the serpent, and it turned into a staff again. I imagine Moses must have thought, "Okay, well thank You, God, but I'm just back to where I started. I'm safe, the snake is gone, but what have I gained from the experience? I'm still standing here, barefoot in the dirt, with my staff."

Moses didn't see this as progress. He had no idea that this was to prepare him for what the magicians of Pharaoh's court were going to pull out of the hat when Moses went before Pharaoh to demand that the Hebrews be released from Egypt. Likewise he had no idea that the whole shepherd gig—leading around a bunch of sheep—was to prepare him for leading a nation, a nation of slaves out of captivity.

God turns failure into freedom. Successful failures.

Freedom to Fill the Road to Heaven

A pastor friend of mind once told me that he remembered as a child seeing his mother cry with tears of joy when the Apollo 13 spacecraft splashed down in the Pacific Ocean. When he asked his mother about her tears, she explained, "I've been praying for those men to return safely, and the Lord has brought them home."

The launch captures our attention, but the splashdown captures our hearts. The joy of seeing an acquaintance, friend, or loved one come to faith can only be eclipsed by the joy that heaven experiences when a person puts their faith in their Creator.

Ultimately, it is the goal of our Savior for each of us to be saved (2 Peter 3:9).

Some may argue that Jesus made things more difficult than they should have been. His life and death were arduous and painful. Not only for Him but His followers as well. Did He and they really have to endure such pain and rejection?

The pain brought about lasting peace, and the rejection brought about redemption.

The vision of the United States president in the early 1960s was to put a man on the moon and return him to Earth safely. Our mission is not merely "to make it to heaven," but to help put as many people on streets of gold as possible.

We are to share freedom with those in need of it.

Several dozen engineers at Mission Control in Houston, Texas inspired a nation with the determination that they would not allow the astronauts to die in space. They would get them home. We must have the same tenacity when praying for our loved ones, friends, and people we meet. We will not allow them to be lost in space. We must get them home. We must get them to heaven.

"His speech persuaded them. They called the apostles in and had them flogged. Then they ordered them not to speak in the name of Jesus, and let them go.

The apostles left the Sanhedrin, rejoicing because they had been counted worthy of suffering disgrace for the Name. Day after day, in the temple courts and from house to house, they never stopped teaching and proclaiming the good news that Jesus is the Christ" (Acts 5:40-42).

Our mission doesn't stop with prayer. We live on Earth not merely for ourselves but for the purpose of helping others get home to heaven safely. This determination and focus will steady each of us to look beyond our own feelings and finish the course.

All of the circumstances in our lives work together to bring about the right results (Romans 8:28). God ensures that any failures are successful failures.

A life focused on the mission of God's will is going to be an adventure. It will have twists and turns. There will be times you'll get knocked off your game plan, but then you can return to the grounding principles God reveals through His Word.

Without question, every aspect of the space program is risky. Astronauts know this going in, but the thrill of the adventure outweighs the fear of death. Life is also risky when you love and care, but is there any other way to live?

Renewal and Revival

Perhaps we could use the words *renewal* and *revival* to distinguish between two key ways we refuel ourselves and others for and during our mission.

If you and I can suffer course corrections, then maybe we can be saved through personal renewal, but for us to find joy in the journey, we must participate in revival, or the saving of others. It is in this transfer of perspective from self to others that we find purpose and significance.

Joseph of the Old Testament had to survive the betrayal of his brothers, slavery in a foreign land, betrayal of his boss's wife, prison, betrayal of fellow prisoners, just to name a few apparent setbacks. But the Lord positioned him through those setbacks to be in a place where he could do more than just be restored (renewal). Joseph was being set up to save millions of lives (physical revival, but you get the idea), not just his own.

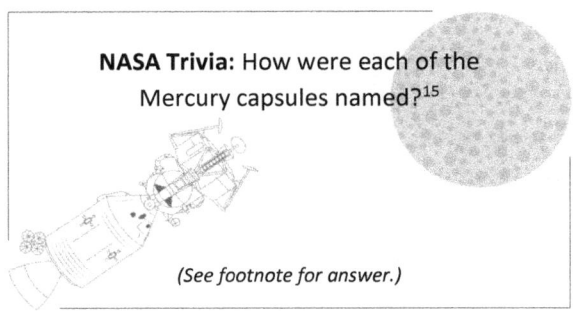

NASA Trivia: How were each of the Mercury capsules named?[15]

(See footnote for answer.)

Our Own "Mission Control Pit Crew"

My observation of the space program over the years has always been a lesson in teamwork. If a driver needs a pit crew to help him keep his race car running at peak performance, how much more does a spacecraft need a committed team? I've always been amazed at how completely the astronauts trust their teams. I never saw or heard an astronaut tell Mission Control that they were not going to take their advice or that they did not see it that way. It was a collaboration of talent and tenacity, but most of all, trust.

There are few things, if any, in life that are more important than the final destination of people's souls. To accomplish a positive mission, we must trust the helps that God has given us. We must trust the Word of God. Even when it doesn't make sense to our situation, we will never go wrong trusting its advice.

---

[15] Each astronaut named his own capsule. He then added the numeral "7" to signify the original astronauts and their dedication to teamwork.

We must trust the Spirit of God and the family of God. No single person is perfect, but together we are made strong. We must come together, despite our faults and our weaknesses, and strengthen one another.

When I was in high school, I took a psychology class that was very interactive. Our teacher taught different concepts using group participation. One exercise I'll never forget was an exercise that she introduced to teach trust.

She had us gather in circles, and one by one each of us had to stand straight and then fall back without looking. The others in our group would catch us. We had to trust them. It was uncanny how difficult it was for us to trust our fellow classmates.

The Bible makes it clear that there is strength in unity. If I'm going to succeed and if you're going to succeed, it will be because we trust not only in Jesus but also other dedicated Christians. Each other.

"How could one man chase a thousand, or two put ten thousand to flight . . . ?" (Deuteronomy 32:30a).

"'But if he will not listen, take one or two others along, so that "every matter may be established by the testimony of two or three witnesses"'" (Matthew 18:16).

"'For where two or three come together in My name, there am I with them'" (Matthew 18:20).

Jesus modeled this principle. It seems crazy, but Jesus trusted the gospel in the hands of, for the most part, uneducated Galilean fishermen. He taught them and He trusted them. He ascended and went into heaven while they were still trying to figure out what was going on (Acts 1).

It is a challenge for every leader to trust his or her team. It is a challenge for every athlete to trust his or her team. It is a challenge for every Christian to trust his or her team. If we stumble, we must trust our team to help us get back up. If we face an unexpected storm in life, know that God has placed a team of people and precepts from the Word of God to help us. Trust the Book. Trust the principles of God's Holy Word. And trust your faith-filled "pit crew." They will not fail you. They will not let you fall.

Jerry Woodfill said, "I could write another hundred accounts of specific acts which, had they not been done, could have resulted in disaster. There was an unseen 'cloud of helpers' whom I now know helped just as much as I did, though they were never recognized. These folks weren't even NASA employees or affiliated with the supporting contractors, Grumman (GAEC), or North American Aviation (NAA)."

Woodfill's reference to a "cloud of helpers" reminds me of a Scripture passage that says we have a "cloud of witnesses."

"Therefore, since we are surrounded by such a great cloud of witnesses, let us throw off everything that hinders and the sin that so easily entangles, and let us run with perseverance the race marked out for us" (Hebrews 12:1).

I think "cloud" may be more than just a descriptive term for a large amount. I think it also could represent the fact that sometimes our strength is unseen.

Plus, we have our own "Mission Control pit crews."

If we put men on the moon, we should be able to get men and women to heaven. One thing we know for sure when it comes to spiritual pursuits is that if you and I and others get safely home to heaven, it will be a team effort.

Paul, writing to the church in Rome, spoke about the necessity of having a team of spiritual support around us.

"How, then, can they call on the one they have not believed in? And how can they believe in the one of whom they have not heard? And how can they hear without someone preaching to

them? And how can they preach unless they are sent? As it is written, 'How beautiful are the feet of those who bring good news!'" (Romans 10:14-15).

There are several facts we know about the team that we need to make it to heaven.

We need the Word of God.

We need the Spirit of God.

We need a pastor.

We need a church.

Our friends who support us are also a strength, but they are not going to be the deciding factor of we make it to heaven or not. We must have those spiritual helps that God has placed in our lives to help us make it home.

Paul was wise enough in his letter to the church at Corinth to know that he was part of a team effort.

"I planted the seed, Apollos watered it, but God made it grow" (1 Corinthians 3:6).

Paul was saying that he recognized that he was only a part of the salvation process. It helps each of us to understand that our role in sharing the gospel with others is to be a team player. Recognize that God will use many different people and avenues to strengthen the body of Christ.

The numerous unsung heroes who worked in non-visible cubicles around the clock were a valuable part of the rescue team for Apollo 13. The same could be said of our mission in life. There are numerous unsung heroes of faith who strengthen each step. A "cloud of witnesses." Not always seen, but often felt.

On July 23, 1969, the last night before splashdown of Apollo 11, the space mission that took man to the moon for the very first time, Neil Armstrong, Buzz Aldrin, and Michael Collins, the three astronauts, made a television broadcast in which Collins commented the following.

"... The Saturn V rocket which put us in orbit is an incredibly complicated piece of machinery, every piece of which worked flawlessly. ... We have always had confidence that this equipment will work properly. All this is possible only through the blood, sweat, and tears of a number of people. ... All you see is the three of us, but beneath the surface are thousands and thousands of others, and to all of those, I would like to say, 'Thank you very much.'"

Aldrin added, "This has been far more than three men on a mission to the moon; more, still, than the efforts of a government and industry team; more, even, than the efforts of one nation. We feel that this stands as a symbol of the insatiable curiosity of all mankind to explore the unknown. ... Personally, in reflecting on the events of the past several days, a verse from Psalms comes to mind. 'When I consider the heavens, the work of Thy fingers, the moon and the stars, which Thou hast ordained; what is man that Thou art mindful of him?'"

Armstrong concluded, "The responsibility for this flight lies first with history and with the giants of science who have preceded this effort; next with the American people, who have, through their will, indicated their desire; next with four administrations and their Congresses, for implementing that will; and then, with the agency and industry teams that built our spacecraft, the Saturn, the *Columbia*, the *Eagle*, and the little EMU, the spacesuit and backpack that was our small spacecraft out on the lunar surface. We would like to give special thanks to all those Americans who built the spacecraft; who did the construction, design, the tests, and put their hearts and all their abilities into those craft. To those people tonight, we give a special thank you, and to all the other people that are listening and watching tonight, God bless you. Good night from Apollo 11."

On April 24, that spacecraft would burn through the ring of fire that circles our Earth and land in the Pacific Ocean. My good friend John Wolfram would be the first diver in the water as a special Navy frogman. He quickly attached a sea anchor to keep the capsule from drifting in the high seas. He was the first human to greet the astronauts upon their return from the moon. He was part of that team.

I've also seen John a number of times, in America and in Asia, help someone make it "home" safely, at a church altar or on a street corner, once again attaching a life anchor called the Word of God to steady their walk and secure their steps.

We've baptized people in barrels and in swimming pools in Vietnam. Together we've preached and prayed with people whose language we did not understand. Just another part of that "cloud of witnesses" who desire to be on the team and help secure a safe return.

America had a team of people who came together and figured out how to accomplish a safe return for three endangered astronauts. Faithful people came together, God reached out with miracles, and the astronauts returned to Earth in a relatively gentle splashdown. God turned failures into successes.

Why did God allow anything at all to go wrong with this spacecraft? Why didn't the mission simply unfold without a problem? On the other hand, why did He allow the astronauts to survive? I believe a few of His reasons may have been to remind the world of His living presence; His miraculous involvement; His infinite love; and to remind us all that He always hears, and often answers, the prayers of those who trust in and rely on Him.

Usually His miracles are small, one-on-one. On occasion they are large enough for the entire globe to witness, in order to once again erase doubts of His presence or His ability to step in and involve Himself in men's activities on (and near) Earth. From human failures, God makes successes.

In 2010, years after the flight was over, Jerry Woodfill, a NASA engineer who had been a leader on the team, contributed to an article called "13 Things That Saved Apollo 13" (http://www.universetoday.com/62339/13-things-that-saved-apollo-13/). This article inspired the book in your hands. I pray this book inspires you.

Go, and make disciples of all nations. Go, and lead the lost home.

Filling the road to heaven is sure to be an adventure, one for the books.

"Far better is it to dare mighty things,
to win glorious triumphs,
even though checkered by failure
than to rank with those poor spirits
who neither enjoy much nor suffer much,
because they live in a gray twilight
that knows not victory nor defeat."
—*Theodore Roosevelt*

Bibliography

Gladwell, Malcom. *David and Goliath*. New York: Little, Brown and Company, 2013.
Webb, Brandon. *The Red Circle*. New York: St. Martin's Paperbacks, 2012.

http://history.nasa.gov/SP-4029/Apollo_13h_Timeline.htm
http://www.universetoday.com/62339/13-things-that-saved-apollo-13/
http://www.spaceacts.com/apollo_13_co2_filter.htm
http://www.spaceacts.com/notanoption.htm
http://www.spaceline.org/flightchron/apollo13.html
http://www.airspacemag.com/need-to-know/how-hot-was-apollo-13-on-reentry-22877442/?no-ist
http://www.universetoday.com/77070/how-cold-is-space/

About the Author

David Myers is the senior pastor of the First Pentecostal Church in Palm Bay, Florida and a constitutional law advocate defending churches and ministries whose religious liberties are being challenged.

In 1994 he graduated Summa Cum Laude with a Bachelor's degree in Systematic Theology from Southeastern University.

In 1997 he studied at Oxford University in Oxford, England. In 1998 he studied at Trinity College in Dublin, Ireland under U.S. Supreme Court Justice Antonin Scalia, and in 1999, at McGill College in Montreal, Canada under U.S. Supreme Court Chief Justice William Rehnquist.

In 2000 he graduated Cum Laude with a Juris Doctorate degree from Barry University School of Law.

In 2001 he went to work for Liberty Counsel, a nonprofit educational and legal defense group working to preserve religious freedom, the sanctity of life, and traditional marriage in America. He cohosted *Law and Justice* and *Faith and Freedom*, national media programs, with Mat Staver. He was part of a team that defended the Ten Commandments at the U.S. Supreme Court.

In 2011 David authored and released the best-selling book *The Supremacy Clause: The Laws of Man That Reveal the Love of God*.

As senior pastor of First Pentecostal, the church has flourished with accelerated revival and numerical growth, including four satellite campuses.

David travels extensively, having visited and ministered in more than one hundred countries as the president of Hands for Healing International, Inc. His passion includes reaching third-world countries with humanitarian relief, construction projects, and spiritual renewal.

David and his wife, Aimee, are blessed with identical twin sons, Gregory and Luke, and a beautiful daughter, Sophia.

Visit him online at www.fpcpalmbay.com, or follow him on Twitter at @dmyers8664.

www.ingramcontent.com/pod-product-compliance
Lightning Source LLC
Chambersburg PA
CBHW070603100426
42744CB00006B/383